THE RESTORATION OF OUR REPUBLIC

**How to Declare Independence from
Party Politics, Special Interests, Mob Democracy,
and Money-Power to Reestablish Freedom and
Liberty in America**

"And I will restore thy judges as at the first, and thy
counselors as at the beginning: afterwards thou
shalt be called, The city of righteousness,
the faithful city."
Isaiah 1:26

About the Author

Farley Merril Anderson, age fifty, lives in the beautiful mountain community of Paradise, Utah. Happily married to his loving and supporting wife, Helen, for over twenty-five years, he is the father of eleven children. For the past eight years, much of his passion and work has centered on the concepts and principles of this, his third book. His previous books are *Nature's Answer- Replenish the Earth,* and *The Book of Revelation Today.* He has also scripted and produced a documentary movie about civil defense. Problems with our current political system were witnessed first-hand as his father, Hartley Anderson, made an unsuccessful bid for the U.S. Senate. Mr. Anderson has been very active in church, civic, community, and family affairs. He has held many volunteer church positions, especially involving teaching both youth and adults, has held many positions within the Boy Scouting organization, conducted primary agricultural research and been vice president of a family-owned nutritional products company. He has been a very popular speaker on the circuit with the National Health Foundation. Hobbies have included scuba, adopting, training and writing about mustang horses, hiking, and enjoying the scenic beauty of America. He is interested in all things historical, especially biographical, and seeking to understand and incorporate great truths, both political and religious, that are our heritage.

TABLE OF CONTENTS

Book Theme, Honoring Christ
The judgment seat (all political positions) ultimately belongs to
Christ. Filling His seat in His absence in a way that honors Him,
is how we best prepare for His return.
Our prayer and goal is that His Kingdom will come and that His
will is done on Earth as it is in Heaven.

Dedication
This book is dedicated with love to our first political chief judge,
George Washington. If all men were as Washington, a
restoration would never be necessary.
In a prayer and a spirit of gratitude, I, at one time asked that love
and appreciation be carried to Washington, that he might know
that the love of liberty yet burns within us, and that we yet
cherish the cause that he gave so much to further. A surprising
thing happened. I felt the great love of this man coming back,
but it came back with an admonition. "Now it is your turn." I
hope at some future date to meet this great man, and be able to
say that we also bore the torch with dignity.

Special Thanks
This book would not have been possible without the efforts of
many unselfish and dedicated people who have helped in my
feeble attempts to convey into words what is in my heart.
Listening ears, focused attention, communication skills and other
help have been generously given. Much of this help has come
from within my own loving and supporting family. My wife, the
love of my life, has been, and always is there. My children, my
greatest teachers, have grown up to also be my helpers, typing,
editing, and giving invaluable feedback. Thanks to my many
friends who have tolerated and helped me, even with my faults
and quirks. Lastly, this book is not something that can be
claimed as mine; so much help came, line upon line and precept
upon precept, with guidance, inspiration and help, to one
attempting a work much beyond myself.

OVERVIEW

Saving our Republic and constitution requires something more powerful than what "is". What "is" is destroying what ought to "be". From our nation's birth, three factors have proved powerful enough to overcome entrenched political evil, public apathy, and even marching and determined redcoats. The same factors are needed today.

These factors are:

1. God, the author of liberty, eternal and unchangeable, waiting to be called upon in faith

2. The call to serve, answered by citizen and leader alike.

3. Correct principles in action.

Our nation is being destroyed by selfishness, especially in high places. Can we rise above our own selfishness? If so, then we can also regain power to call the unselfish (those not seeking just their own will) and the best qualified to lead. This call, answered by both citizen and leader alike can save our Republic. Our political goal should be to follow the will of God. Then we call to service those who also have this same goal. This leads us toward His kingdom come on earth as it is in heaven. Opposite of the call to serve, we see the followers of evil promoting their own selves, objectives, and self-interests.

Christ and the Devil operate differently

We see from the study of truth the difference between good and evil. The ultimate expression of good, the Son of God, was called and chosen by God. Christ came, not to do His own will, but the will of Him who sent Him (John 5:30). Thus the Father honored the Son. This is our pattern. We honor Christ by striving to do his will. Our hope in Christ is He will then honor us by establishing His Kingdom on Earth. Much of His Kingdom come on Earth as it is in Heaven is done through His servants on Earth. We recognize that ultimately all political power (the judgment seat) belongs to Christ.

Christ's power comes from his honor. Christ is so

honorable; all that is good seeks to obey his voice. Christ shares his power with those who become honorable like him. The Declaration of Independence declares that governments derive their just powers from the consent of the governed. It is believed that even the government of heaven receives authority to rule by this consent. In God's kingdom, people are led, not forced or coerced. Christ's life and work was an invitation to follow. Our rule in God's kingdom is over things, not people.

The Devil obtains his power from being a liar, an accuser, and deceiver (Revelation 12:7). The Devil and Earthly followers want power over us. By taking things, they can control people. History shows that political disciples of the deceiver (false prophets and saviors) promote themselves to obtain power. They promise an earthly utopia and security, but ultimately deliver Hell on Earth. Politics have a powerful pull for those seeking to promote themselves. Currently, self-promotion is the heart and core of our established politics.

A change is possible

Is there an alternative to the deceitful, power-seeking, self-promotional and accusatory nature of our political establishment? To restore the structure of our house, we do not begin by changing the shingles. We start at the foundation. The foundation of our nation has been eroded and undermined. The call to serve by a people, who individually reverence God as the ultimate source of all that is good, rebuilds and restores freedom's foundation. This is how God can restore our judges (political leaders) as at the first, preceding a return to righteousness (Isaiah 1:26). The call to serve raises the bar for our political leaders by choosing those not promoting their own selfish interests.

The call to serve by itself, however, is not enough. It must be combined with correct principles and be blessed from on high to overcome what lurks from below. We must recognize that an ultimate truth and right does exist, and seek to align ourselves with it. The humility of recognizing this truth can become our strength and ultimately the strength of our nation.

The Political Alternative

Imagine a reversal in current politics. Now politicians stand in front of thousands and say whatever will get them elected. This is followed by little input from citizens until the next election. Alternatively, thousands could be organized and called to serve, searching out and supporting the best and most qualified. These candidates could then be put before the ratifying vote of the people. This could be a system of participation that helps, watches, evaluates, gives feed-back, and trains through service. Organization is important to make the call both successful and meaningful. We can follow the Biblical principle, calling many, from which we choose the few (Matthew 20:16, 22:14 Revelation 17:14). We could choose from all participants those who are the most prepared, whose life has been most honorable, and whose hearts are not set upon the honors of men or the things of the world. We could have such a system. This system would promote those who are the most skilled at service and selflessness, instead of those who are the most skilled at flattery and selfishness. It can happen. We have an opportunity to change politics. This book is about those who answer the call. This book is about you.

BEGINNINGS

We can restore the political character of America when we learn what it means to say, "This is my country, I am responsible for my government. I will participate and serve to keep citizen government alive. I will value freedom and liberty, allowing the pursuit of happiness more than the politician's promise of unearned ease, security, or wealth. I will join other like-minded Americans and make it so." We will then discover that we are part of a divine mandate. We are children of the promise. We face Goliath problems, but our God is a God of miracles. Sometimes these miracles are as simple as smooth stones in a shepherd's sling. What is needed is the courage to go forth, achieving God's glory for what can be. The miracle starts with you.

Awakening

A great manipulation has given the power of the political process to politicians. This power is supported by party politics, special interest, mob democracy and money power. A prideful profanity, a worship of false gods is destroying America. If we allow any man-made standard to replace what we know of God's law as a basis for decisions, this pride becomes a false god. Our political system is overrun by this pride. We see this infection most clearly in four areas: Party politics, Special Interests, Mob democracy, and Money Power.

Definitions:

- **Party Politics.** The political party becomes the standard for right. Power flows from the party. Those who want power fall in line behind or push themselves in front of a political party, regardless of right or wrong.

- **Special Interests.** Seeking to beg, borrow, or steal votes and power to selfishly promote their special interests without regard to justice, the ultimate good, or the higher principles of revealed truth.

- **Mob Democracy.** The majority becomes the god that rules. Anything is right so long as the majority agrees; be it plunder, injustice, evil or just plain wrong.

- **Money Power.** The political system is for sale. As with cheap wine, it causes people to become drunk, addicted, lose their morals, and fall into a deep sleep while their souls, and the soul of the nation, are robbed and plundered.

An awakening can restore real power to the people. We call this awakening the Independence Movement. Today's problems have been foretold, but so also, deliverance. We choose the future. The world around us continues to degrade, even as many personally strive to live a good life and make a difference. Good people tend to keep themselves busy pursuing a full and happy life and naturally expect this if others. It is just as natural however, for those seeking power and unjust gain to combine and organize to achieve their goals of oppression and control. "All that is necessary for the triumph of evil is that good men to do nothing." (Edmund Burke) If we simply allow those who want power and position to rule and "do it for us" we will get the government we deserve. It took the power of organization and unity, coupled with an underlying goodness to give us a free and independent nation. The call for organization and unity for good is just as urgent today.

America is a miracle

God is the author of our history. The American miracle began with a special recognition of God as our Father. As a new religious reformation known as the Great Awakening swept this continent, (1740 to 1760) God prepared His people to do a great political work. The work was to raise an entire nation to accept the principles of self-rule (individual sovereignty) and to become a nation of Kings unto God. This miracle required a physical and spiritual separation from the power and politics of Europe. We have been the benefactors of that change.

Blessings of Individual sovereignty

As people accepted responsibilities, blessings soon followed. We enjoy blessings of freedom, liberty, opportunity, and control over our own destiny that far surpass anything even great kings of the past have known. We can open our garage door and have a powerful modern chariot at our instant beckon and control. We can travel further and faster across more borders than any king of the past. We enjoy a variety of food, culture, entertainment, education, and opportunity, in excess of the highest nobility in bygone ages. The great miracle is that God made blessings of kings available to everyone in the entire nation as we accepted the responsibility of self-rule.

The sad reality is that if we reject the responsibilities, we will also lose the blessings. The temptation is to let go of the responsibilities God wants for us, his children, to receive as a prelude to blessings. Give up the responsibilities and the blessings quickly evaporate. We cannot have blessings without responsibilities.

Those advocating a system of degeneration under the guise that they will "take care of us" are inspired from a different source than God. The Father wants us to follow His Son and also become kings and priests unto Him. (Revelation 1:6, 5:10, 20:6, 21:7). God ultimately wants his children to grow up to be like him. We cannot grow up if we do not accept the responsibilities associated with the growth.

Great history is being made today

We are empowered with the ability to vote. While this power has been trivialized by the power and influence of party politics, special interests, mob democracy, and money power, the real power is still with the people. We have not lost the ability to say "no" to wrong and "yes" to right. We can go within the political parties of America and offer a change so refreshing and natural that the inertia of fear, the pollution of corruption, and the confusion of disunity will sway as the grass before a great wind. This book is about the changes necessary so that our vote can make a difference. The mechanism for this change is simple and direct. It can be explained in a very few words. The implications are so great that modern sophistry can and will be replaced with clear and correct thought and action.

We can recruit and support our best people to represent us, putting them ahead of usurpers. The work and effort to organize and accomplish tasks at this early stage is many times more effective than trying to be heard by politicians after their election. The great part is that this work, fueled by a quest for what is great about America, becomes in and of itself part of a great redemption. This is not a new political party, (although it could be) but rather a more representative way to issue the call to serve, coupled with citizen support, input, and evaluation.

Washington and Jefferson knew

The greatness of America stems from its goodness. This is so central; it still powers the greatest nation and the freest people that the world has ever known. This goodness is being lulled to sleep by the influence of darkness and fatigue. The slumber is not synonymous with the morbidity of death. Most Americans are amazed to learn our nation's Founding Fathers tried to establish something better than our current political party system and politics. In Washington's Farewell Address, he warned us against the inherit evils of party politics. The Founding Fathers warned us against the injustices of what was referred to as the spoils system. Jefferson's political model of just representation is painfully needed today. Jefferson was always the student of history, both scriptural and secular. He based his model upon ancient biblical law and what he considered the last remaining framework of that structure. This is seen in the foundation of European common law, handed down from the Anglo-Saxons. The journey back, while perilous and difficult, is nothing more than the quest for home.

Self-rule is possible when we rise above our fallen nature

A yearning and reaching for that which is Heavenly can be coupled, or married, with a merciful redemption of God's love. John Adams said, "Our Constitution is made only for a moral and religious people. It is wholly inadequate to the government of any other". A man who acts like a tyrant over his domain will lose the opportunity to experience a likeness of Heaven on Earth.

A strange and miraculous phenomenon is that we receive more by giving than by taking. Each of us is faced with temptation to unrightly take. If we are willing to take from government, we lose the independence of self-rule and elect immoral leaders. These leaders then utilize the power of position to consolidate their power, take all they can, and hide their sins. This is the birthplace of oppression. We are judged even in the here and now by how we choose to judge (Matthew 7:2). The cost of not being involved in government is not always immediately apparent.

Something must be done

Most Americans feel a special yearning and reverence for the Constitution of the United States. We know intuitively it was divinely inspired, something wonderfully precious and rare. The Constitution is something we are honor-bound to protect. We are accountable to God who inspired it and to those brave men and women whose blood was sacrificed upon its holy altar.

Most Americans are also painfully aware that the American political system has gone incredibly amuck. The American political system is the moral equivalent of money changers parked within the walls of a holy temple. The time for cleansing has come. Many are conditioned to figuratively think of money changers and the temple as part of the same great whole. We intuitively know, however, one is a Godly thing to be honored, and one is a great evil. Some believe that money changers are, in reality, the temple itself. After cleansing though, it will be obvious that the temple (the Godly Constitution) is based upon the eternal, while the money changers (modern American politics) are nothing more than usurpers. We cannot go back in time, but we can always start over. We can restore our political leaders as at the first.

This book is divided into six sections, each based on an important concept. A principle of just representation will be introduced and the opposition exposed. Once the proper groundwork and foundation has been laid, tremendous political change is possible. This book is about you. This book is about the revolution challenging you and how you can change the world. This is about the discovery that God is speaking to you, calling you forth to do a great work, speaking to you from his holy writ, guiding your path, preparing your way, and working through you, to help answer the prayer given so long ago that His Kingdom come, His will be done, on Earth as it is in Heaven. This is about your discovery. It all depends upon you. With God as our eternal partner, we will never fail.

Becoming Kings and Priests unto God

This book is about sacrifices needed and a great work to be accomplished. This is about a small movement at the helm moving a great ship out of the path of destruction and towards the discovery of a whole new world. This is about learning it must be your hand on the helm. Are you up to the job? Yes, because here you are responding to the call. The great promises are sure. John the Revelator refers to you as a king and a priest unto God (Revelation 1:6, 5:10, 20:6, 21:7). As a priest, you will be involved in the great spiritual work of lifting your brothers and sisters unto God. This is an extension of God's mercy. As a king, you will first become firmly rooted on the principles of self-rule. Second, you help establish the order of Heaven (self-rule and individual sovereignty with limited and restricted government under God). This is an extension of God's justice. This allows the fullest expression of freedom and liberty.

The battlefield of our choosing

In past political battlefields, many of our heroes have emerged bruised, bloodied, and less than victorious. It may be brave to boldly approach a powerful enemy on battlefields of his choice and making, where his weapons are most destructive and terrible. Money, media, status quo, self-promotion, intimidation, pride, arrogance, selfishness, apathy and ignorance are powerful weapons of the adversary. Yet history is full of examples of many "undefeatable foe" vanquished by the common man. We can be as wise as Washington, Jackson, or Houston at their greatest hour, who met the enemy on their terms and the battlefield of their choice. The enemy is vulnerable if drawn into the natural territory of the minds and hearts of people.

LOOKING FORWARD

The basic premise of this book is simple. Namely, a citizens' organization with a foundation of correct principles could completely change our political realities. We can call the best statesmen to serve, eliminating the corrupt campaigning, promising, and obligatory pre-election procedures. Through support and involvement of a citizens' organization during and after the election, we can keep citizen government alive. This book is for every person who has asked, "Why does it have to be this way?" We must care enough to make the difference.

A suggestion for an actual structure of organization that is simple, direct, and powerful is covered at the end of this book. The more difficult part is the change of heart and a return to correct principles. This must be accomplished if the structure is to have meaning.

The six concepts of this book can change hearts

First, look at the promise and hope to see God has a plan for America that is awaiting fulfillment. Next, explore the power of the call to serve verses a system that elects those promising the most because they want power the most. Then look at the inseparably and interrelationships of rights and responsibilities. Following is the contrasts between the power of love verses the love of power. Now prepare for the intellectual challenge of perceiving the eternal nature of the law and how this is the foundation of the restoration needed. Last, realize that without work nothing happens. This work must be organized, efficient, and inspired, to accomplish what is possible. After some final thoughts and conclusions, a simple structure and organization is presented under the heading, "methods and structure, how to start".

Change–a big word–do we desire it?

Our political system needs work, but where do we begin? All great movements are driven by great ideas. This book focuses on six concepts and ideas to empower a movement called the Independence Movement. Following this is a proposal to establish unity of action. These are not new ideas, nor the plan of action untried. Thomas Jefferson believed in the power of a simple system to call our best statesmen to serve. He based his beliefs upon observations from the writing of Moses and the model handed down and proven in action over centuries by the Anglo-Saxons. He believed this structure has the power to fuel a just system of representative government.

The problem with current politics is unbridled selfishness. Isaiah prophesied, "Thy princes are rebellious and the companions of thieves. Everyone loveth gifts, and followeth after rewards". (Isaiah 1:23) **The power of the call to serve is that the interests of citizens are protected through a system to issue the call to those best qualified to protect our rights.** The candidate is supported in the process of being elected and thus is not alone in shouldering the tremendous burden of the election campaign. Also, the candidate is not left alone to take unjust rewards from the power of the position. In all, the sacred marriage covenant between government and people is fostered. People shoulder the responsibility of supporting leaders. Leaders are held accountable to protect the rights of the people. Any movement this direction is an improvement. Envisioned is a massive swing towards a just balance.

Is it possible to go from where we are now back to a simpler and more direct method? The answer is a resounding yes!

America, awake and reclaim your destiny

Arise and shoulder the responsibilities upon which your freedom and liberty reside. We might begin by thinking this could work. As we read and study, we see it can work. Ultimately, this becomes a reality, because we believe and work together to make it happen. All that is needed is good people seeing what can be, and then continue on until it is. This is easier than seems at first. Can we say and believe:

I would participate in a citizen's organization to issue the call for statesmen to serve. So would others.

I would value an organization that watches and supports those called to serve. So would others.

I would support a statesman unencumbered and unpolluted through campaigning, promising, and power seeking. So would others.

I would vote for the best man, offered in the best way, supported by the best people. So would others.

The purpose of this book is to provide a stimulus to create and support the Independence Movement. This movement can restore freedom and liberty by providing a framework for patriotic and freedom-loving people, to focus their resources, energy, time, and talents in a politically significant way.

We can:

A. Set higher standards of political morality, and help each other learn, teach, understand and incorporate correct leadership principles.

B. Create and utilize a simple system to choose from among our ranks the most honorable and best qualified to enter the political arena.

C. Build and strengthen the organization so that power is shifted away from party politics, special interests, mob democracy, and money power and back towards the responsibility of the people.

D. Support publicly-elected officials in the discharge of their duty and give citizen input in an organized, effective, and timely manner. Through this support, raise statesmen.

E. Evaluate what is being done politically by set standards of responsibility. Give clout to this evaluation by means of unity of action and the ability to distribute information.

Working to build support for a movement and organization makes more sense than the same effort put behind a specific candidate. Support for a movement, organization, and a philosophical ideal can build and carry over time, gaining more and more momentum. Support for an individual candidate is limited to term of office.

With no apologies, this book mixes politics and religion

We believe in the concept of the separation of church and state, but this understanding is more akin to that of our nation's founders, meaning no interference with religion by government oppression and no state religion. The banishment of religion (thought, prayer, or influence) from public affairs is a recent phenomenon. The lie "politics and religion don't mix" is told so often many accept this at face value without thinking about whose interest it promotes, or why it is given. If religious and moral people do nothing, tyranny will rise. Evil does not want you or God involved in government, or to notice what is being done. A political system not based or evaluated upon correct principle is dangerous.

When first discussing the need for prayer in congress, Samuel Adams arose and said that he was no bigot and could hear a prayer from any gentleman of piety and virtue who was at the same time a friend to his country.[1] Immediately after the signing of the Declaration of Independence, he revealed its purpose. "We have this day restored the Sovereign to Whom alone men ought to be obedient. He reigns in heaven and...from the rising to the setting sun, may His kingdom come."[2] The glory of a Heaven on Earth would not have been revealed if it was not possible to obtain. We must understand that vision if we are to obtain that reality. Modern study and analysis of the writings and speeches of our Founding Fathers clearly demonstrates that the Bible, even more so than the Constitution, is our nation's

---

[1] Mark A Beliles, Stephen K. McDowell, *America's Providential History* Charlottesville VA, Providence Foundation 1989 pg 133
[2] Ibid P. 148

18

founding document.

A second great awakening will precede a restoration

The restoration of our Republic will be preceded by a re-committal to our religious roots. The influence of religion is the very thing that gave birth and success to the great American experiment. Without the Great Awakening of 1740-1760, there would have been no revolution. Likewise, a second great awakening will precede a restoration. It is entirely appropriate and necessary for religion to influence politics. This influence should be manifest in an organized, responsible, and effective manner. For many years the political drumbeat has been leading the people towards a system designed to dethrone God. We can consciously and actively make a decision to go another direction and leave that destructive system behind.

The glory of America stems from the vision of 1776. We are in decline because of a different vision from a different source. America is not about politicians. Politicians are not entitled to run and ruin the country just because they want to. We must love ourselves enough to demand just representation. We must love our fellow men enough to establish justice. We must love our posterity enough to see and fix the problems of our day while building a foundation to last for a better tomorrow.

The differences between right and wrong involve more than just what we profess to believe on Sunday. Who do we actually choose to follow? We have been forewarned that false saviors (political and spiritual leaders) would be a particular challenge for our day. Furthermore, the warning specifies that these false Christ's and false prophets that would rise (expect them in high places) would be incredibly effective at seducing even the elect if possible (Mark 13:22) (Revelation 12:9).

Christ is our example

The Savior, Christ, is governed by love. He is a Creator. He teaches us to follow him, improve upon all that we do, and put back more than we take. This produces life and growth. Only in a system of creation, can we legitimately give; otherwise we are only taking what someone has else created. God's system produces abundance.

The false savior is governed by hate. As a destroyer, he can only take. This produces a system of shortage and death.

The true Savior offers us the truth that leads to individual freedom and liberty. Christ beckons in peace with a still small voice to follow Him. Metaphorically, we climb the mountain of the Lord towards the light. The higher we climb and closer we get to the light, the greater is our vision and perspective.

The false savior offers lies that lead to collective control and bondage. The Devil shouts in accusation day and night (Revelation 12:10) as he manipulates towards the darkness. The further we descend into the bottomless pit, the dimmer our vision and perspective.

The true Savior lives in honor and was called to serve. He seeks to have the honor, glory, and power returned to the Father. He organizes and calls His followers to do good. This is what built America.

False saviors live in dishonor, yet promote themselves. They seek to have the honor, glory, credit and power for themselves. They combine to do evil. This is what is destroying America.

As it was earlier stated by Samuel Adams, the purpose of the Declaration of Independence was to restore God as our King. This is also the process of restoring the individual sovereignty of the people. We can once again declare our independence and organize for our return to this great cause.

The Parable of the King

Once there was a powerful king, born of noble parents with a great heritage of righteous and prosperous rule. He was talented, strong, just, brave and mighty. All that was necessary for his success was before him. He had but one weakness, his youth and inexperience fostered an inner self-doubt. Could it be

20

that he was really meant for these awesome responsibilities? This self-doubt opened the door for scheming and wicked men to gradually usurp power by promising to take some of the burden and begin to fulfill responsibilities that should have been his. These self-promoting men assured the king of their righteous intent and went to extraordinary effort to cloak their secret works of darkness. On the surface, it appeared he had all the rights and blessing of his position without the responsibility and burden. Wine in abundance, and other opiates, caused him to sleepily ignore more and more obvious signs of trouble. A great and rude awakening came when he realized that he had been sold out. The kingdom was bankrupt, the enemy financed from his own treasury, combined and threatening at the gates, as well as within. The wicked usurpers were claiming the throne. **You are this king.** Give up, or claim your inheritance, rights and responsibilities, even at great peril. You open the great book of the law and find there is a way back.

CONCEPT NUMBER ONE
THE PROMISE AND THE HOPE

"And I will restore thy judges as at the first, and thy counselors as at the beginning: afterward thou shalt be called, The city of righteousness, the faithful city."
-Isaiah 1:26

The first chapter of Isaiah is one of the most politically pertinent chapters in all of scripture. It speaks directly to us today. This wonderful promise (chapter 1 verse 26) is America's promise. Whenever we see a promised blessing from God, we should carefully evaluate the conditions or covenants necessary to claim the promised blessing. Our first political chief judge, President George Washington was called to serve rather than seeking the office himself. This is a pattern and a type (Biblical and secular) of what has been and can be. After much earnest thought, meditation, prayer and desire to discover what could personally be done to save our constitution, a very strong spiritual impression came that this scripture contained the answer. This book is a product of a personal quest to discover what is meant by the restoration of our judges as at the first.

The very first concept of just representation is to have hope in something better. Hope is possible because we recognize the divine promises, see the natural consequences of calling wise leaders to serve, and base our actions upon correct principles.

Anciently, God referred to His people as children of the covenant or promise, meaning that by covenant, certain blessings would follow a particular course of action. America has been the modern keeper of that covenant and the recipient of its rewards. Times are rapidly changing. A revival of America's spirit and destiny will follow a re-commitment to the concepts and works that are the foundation of our nation's greatness. God has shown the way. What first appeared to be just a glimmer of hope from a far horizon is, in reality, a carefully placed beacon of light from the past illuminating a safe pathway home.

God is interested in politics

The Bible explicitly lays the ground work for both spiritual and political peace, harmony, justice, love, service, responsibility, independence, freedom, and liberty. The greatest evidence of this Godly concern is God's Son, the King of Heaven. As a Redeemer, He is coming to bring the order of Heaven to Earth. Our work as God's servants here on earth is to prepare the way for this great marriage.

Somehow many have bought into a great lie that politics has nothing to do with religion and thus religious people should not be involved. If this is true, who wins? It is hoped that the reader will feel of the same spirit of hope and joy felt while this book was being written. A prayer is offered to the Great Author of Liberty. We must seek His forgiveness for where we are, and His aid in our return to what we can become.

The Earth is preparing for a great marriage of Heaven and Earth. The principle of hope starts with looking up. If we look up, we will see God. If we see God, we will begin to see His order. If we see His order, we can begin to establish that order here on earth. It is a great eternal principle that as we look up, things will look up.

TRUE RELIGION—The purpose of true religion is to teach correct principles, and lead us toward redemption so we can govern ourselves. We then use this agency to lift ourselves and others.

CORRECT GOVERNMENT—The purpose of correct government is to protect our rights so we can practice true religion.

True religion and correct government are the basis of God's work with man on Earth. It is a process by which God lifts his children. Freedom and liberty are the foundations of true religion and correct government. Without them, the progress of God's children is damned (or held back) by the enemy of righteousness.

After much thought, pondering, and prayer, here is a

simple, useable definition of both Freedom and Liberty. This will help us reason together.

Freedom; *Lack of oppression* In common use we say freedom from...and then list an oppression. Freedom is the spiritual quality of being able to progress towards a worthy goal. Ultimately, all freedom stems from the fact that God chooses not to oppress His children. God gives agency (the ability to rightfully use his creation) to man. Freedom is spread when this light inspires God's children to do likewise. Freedom is based upon independence (in individuals as well as nations). Independence comes only when we are ready, willing and able to accept the responsibilities upon which the independence is based. We cannot be free while expecting others to take care of the responsibilities of our independence.

Satan knows that the quickest way to lose our freedom is to become irresponsible, thus losing our independence and with it the power to progress towards our worthy goals.

Liberty; *The physical quality of being able to move and act within society*. In common usage we say liberty to...and then list one of the abilities we have to move and act within society. The greatest liberty is under the order of God. Liberty comes because there is peace, and peace is possible only when the principles of justice prevail. Justice means that we treat other people the way we want to be treated (Matthew 7:12).

The quickest way to destroy liberty is to become unjust (the classic definition of sin) and thus destroy peace. Where there is no peace, the ability to move and act within a society is curtailed. Where there is no peace, the order of God is not possible and thus there is no liberty. The Devil knows and uses this also. In fact, he became the Devil and was cast out of Heaven because he was unjust and irresponsible.

Discovering life's purpose

God's children are on earth to learn by first-hand experience (the greatest teacher) the difference between God and the Devil and demonstrate our ability to make wise choices based upon this knowledge. It really is this simple. The Law (every just law and all the commentary on it) and all the prophets (every inspired word ever written or uttered) can be summarized as "Love the Lord (and His order) with all our hearts and love our neighbors as ourselves" (Matthew 22:37-40). Love is the greatest principle. As we love the Lord and seek His order we achieve liberty. As we love our neighbors as ourselves, we become responsible and thus achieve freedom.

Love is all about service. We love whom we serve. Christ, who has the greatest love, offered the greatest service. Two of the greatest works of service we are to be involved in are summarized as, true religion and correct government. We have freedom because of God's mercy. The Earth is supplied by God with every necessity for man to live in a sphere of independence, if he acts responsibly. This is because God in his power and wisdom chooses not to oppress man. We obtain liberty as we accept God's order based upon justice. The liberty is kept in place because of peace based upon justice among men. God's order is established by God's children becoming self-ruling and sovereign in justice under God. Freedom and liberty are possible because God is just and merciful. Man must also become just and merciful (the definition of righteousness) to have and keep freedom and liberty.

Responsibilities of self-rule are sacred and must be guarded

We only delegate to government those limited powers necessary to secure peace based upon the principles of justice. If we are to have freedom, we must eliminate government oppression that man may have independence based upon his acceptance of responsibility. This is the security that allows the pursuit of happiness.

The light is going out in America because we are moving away from the light. The Devil was cast out of the light by choices he made. We likewise can make the very same choices. If we want the light to return to America, we must make choices that move us towards the light. The light is in a fixed position. It is us that must be moving. Remember salvation is not about what happens to the world, but rather about individual choices we make. It is fair to say it really is all up to us. Choose ye this day whom ye will serve.

We face difficult and complex problems. Often we overlook simple answers because we are looking beyond the mark. We get too busy fighting alligators to drain the swamp. We are at an end of time. This is either good or bad news. If we have had enough of the way things are and really want to be part of something much better, then this is the best of times. The great adventure begins now. If we are part of the problem, well, the days of power are numbered. If we only wish things could get better but have lost hope then we too are part of the problem and are committing the gravest of sins. If we recognize sin we can begin to repent. If we repent quickly, God is quick to forgive. Forgiveness is rooted in hope. Hope turns to faith which motivates us to action. Thus, faith can and will move mountains. If we are seeking hope, we will find hope in abundance in God's word.

The Time of Reckoning

The greatest commentary about our time comes to us through the scriptures. Particularly pertinent to our day are the writings of Isaiah and John the Revelator. Both were prophets at an end of a time. Isaiah was the last prophet to speak to the combined nation of Israel before the destruction and bondage of the ten tribes, and John was the last remaining apostle of the Messianic era. Both prophesied of a time of separation. They foresaw great future judgments coming upon the wicked of our day, while the repentant, faithful and righteous were to be miraculously delivered. Both were prophetically filled with empathy for our day as we face similar challenges to those of their day. They wrote for us. Other ways for describing this end of time is: "A day of judgment", "Times of Ripeness", "Harvest", and "Time of Reckoning". On one hand, we face a day of destruction, vengeance, wrath, burning, suffering, death, bondage, and darkness. On the other hand, we can choose deliverance, guidance, comfort, miracles, and light. When the end comes, these are the only choices. The middle ground is gone. There are no greater prophesies of destruction in all scripture than those described by Isaiah and John the Revelator. There are no greater promises of blessing in all scripture than those described by Isaiah and John the Revelator. In both cases their writing refers to our day. These words of Isaiah from his first chapter speak directly to us. (Words in parenthesis added)

> Come now, and let us reason together, saith the Lord: though your sins be as scarlet, they shall be white as snow; though they be red (Marxist and socialistic) like crimson, they shall be as wool. If ye be willing and obedient, ye shall eat of the good of the land: But if ye refuse and rebel, ye shall be devoured with the sword: For the mouth of the Lord hath spoken it. How is the faithful city become a harlot! It was full of judgment; righteousness lodged in it; but now murderers. Thy silver (constitutional money) is become dross (base metals), thy wine mixed with water (inflated money); Thy princes (politicians) are rebellious, and companions of thieves: every one loveth gifts, and followeth after rewards:… And I will turn my hand upon thee, and purely purge away thy dross… And I will restore thy Judges (political leaders) as at the first, and thy counselors as at the beginning: afterward thou shalt be called, the city of righteousness, the faithful city. Zion (America) shall be redeemed with judgment, and her converts with righteousness. And the destruction of the transgressors and of the sinners shall be together, and they that forsake the Lord shall be consumed.
>
> (Isaiah 1:18-23, 25-28)

Christ comes when we are ready to receive Him

Some Christians may believe that the present system is the best we can hope for until He whose right it is to reign returns. They may even think that not being involved politically is scripturally sanctioned. This is a grave error.

John the Revelator clearly teaches that the Savior comes when "His bride (His people) hath made herself ready...arrayed in fine linen, clean and white, for the fine linen is the righteousness of the saints...blessed are they which are called unto the marriage supper of the Lamb" (Revelation 19:7-9). Jesus Christ is our King and our High Priest. Both of these roles are vital to the great redeeming work of our Lord. Many failed to recognize the Savior in Biblical times because they were solely looking for a physical Redeemer. They failed to recognize Christ in His role as High Priest and spiritual leader. They were only looking for a king. Many people in our day are solely looking for the spiritual and may be blind to the Savior coming as King as well as our great High Priest. The highest form of worship of our Lord is to "come and follow Him", to emulate Him, to become like Him (1 John 3:2). John teaches that Jesus Christ hath made us kings and priests unto God and His Father (Revelation 1:6, 5:10, 20:6, 21:7). Thus we are taught that not only is the Lord, our great example, working for both the spiritual and physical/political, but we also are to be involved in the very same great work.

Being a king under Christ, the High King

We are granted our individual sovereignty within God's kingdom. Thus, God grants agency to man. God's rule is self-rule. This is the higher order of the coming kingdom. The concept of individual sovereignty was clearly understood by the Founding Fathers of this nation. It has been stated that the unofficial motto of the American Revolution was "No King but King Jesus." The concept of individual sovereignty seems to be all but lost in modern times. We will restore this principle as a gift to present to our coming Lord.

The principle of individual sovereignty is centered in love. As an inalienable right (a gift from God) the acceptance of individual sovereignty is the greatest act of loving ourselves. As a principle of justice, protecting the individual sovereignty of our neighbors is the greatest act of loving our neighbors. The concept of individual sovereignty means that in reality we are a nation of kings and queens under God. This is the intent of our American Constitution. To see clearly the balance between the Heavenly principles of order and agency, following is a model.

Heavenly principles of individual sovereignty centered on love.

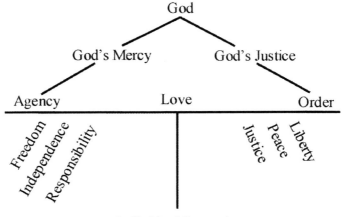

On the left side of the model is agency under God. On the right side is order under God. Both are complementary principles when balanced by love, which must be followed to achieve individual sovereignty. We can look at the world around us to see what order without love looks and feels like, or unbridled agency without love. It's not pretty. Notice how freedom is built upon independence, which flows from responsibility, liberty stems from peace, established upon justice. The base line represents the Kingdom of Heaven. This is the Kingdom we seek to establish on Earth.

It is worth while to ponder the relationships between the spiritual and physical. The spiritual governs the physical. The physical provides a base and supports the spiritual. This is as the Heavens should govern the Earth and the Earth makes it possible for man to stand and reach towards the Heavens. As you look upon the illustration, see the balance between freedom and liberty, independence and peace, responsibility and justice. All is held in place by love. Love is the greatest commandment.

Eternal laws are at work here. If we sense a loss of freedom, we look to see how independence and responsibility are being undermined. If liberty is curtailed, we look to the reestablishment of peace by correcting the underlying injustice. Everything must be balanced by love, which is the basis of individual sovereignty.

Only love has the power to balance order and agency

Without love, order will crush agency, or agency will undermine and collapse order. Love has the power to bring the Heavenly order to Earth. It is important to realize our own self-interest in upholding freedom and liberty in love. Protection of self-interest is a basic correct tenant of our American system. Self-interest should not be confused with selfishness, which is driven by enmity and is destructive to both freedom and liberty. Ultimately it is always in our self-interest to do what is right. Likewise, in spite of short term gains, selfishness or wrong behavior is always self-destructive.

Overcoming opposition

Many people are disgusted with politics and fear there is no possibility for real reform given the current political situation. They are right in that the current system has become corrupt so that the type of change necessary cannot occur via the present political situation. They are wrong if they believe that we cannot change the situation. The majesty of God's law is coming to America![3] New hope will occur with basic change based on eternal principles of good. Nothing is so powerful as an idea whose time has come. Great truths combined with eternal faith at times of urgent need are unstoppable.

What of opposition? A basic tenant of our Earthly experience is opposition in all things. There is a system based upon hatred and the loss of individual sovereignty. Freedom and liberty are not a part of this system. Peace is replaced with fear. Instead of independence we see dependence and control. The hallmark of this system is the basic lack of individual

---

[3] W. Cleon Skousen, *The Majesty of God's Law*, Salt Lake City, Utah Ensign publishing 1996 pg.1

responsibility. Its injustice is driven by its central hatred. It is a system authored by the great last-days false prophet, Karl Marx. It is called communism and socialism. Scarlet red is its banner. Both openly and subtly these doctrines are destroying America.

Marx as a great false prophet

To see Marx as a false prophet requires the intellectual effort to see beyond the stereotype of a bearded vagabond carrying a sign that reads, "The world ends tomorrow." Infinitely more damaging to a free people is the false promises of utopia that leads to the establishment of Hell on Earth. These are the satanic lies that bind men down with the chains of Hell.

There is false hope promised by the socialists and communists (given by the father of lies) of a light at the end of their tunnel. These systems have been around long enough that we can now judge them by their fruits. We see that the only light emanating from this bottomless pit is from the dingy lamps of slaves toiling to enlarge the tomb.

In all of scripture, no more politically pertinent chapter exists than the very first chapter of Isaiah. An exact and accurate description of our day is given. The entire book of Isaiah is prophecy. Political, spiritual, and physical status parallel our day. Isaiah was the last prophet to testify to the combined nation of Israel before a great division and separation. This was a time when the people had forgotten God and His law. Part of the people, the ten tribes, continued on and were enslaved, driven, and destroyed. The rest of Israel changed direction and repented under King Hezekiah. They were miraculously delivered. This is a type of what we can expect for our day.

In the first chapter of Isaiah, there is a wonderful prophecy for our day. Seldom is this scripture quoted in the political context of the chapter, but let's do so now.

"Come now, and let us reason together, saith the Lord: though your sins be as scarlet, they shall be as white as snow; though they be red like crimson, they shall be as wool (Isaiah 1:18)."

To what are the Red sins referring? Remember the political context of the chapter. Remember that the red dragon (the devils pre-earthly organization) was cast out of Heaven to this earth (Revelation chapter 12). The Earthly followers of the devil are also drawn to this red banner. Communists, Nazis and others have used bright red as an identifying mark.

It is time now for the valiant to step up and cast out our red (Marxist and socialist) national and personal sins. The key as to how this is to be accomplished is given in Isaiah 1:25-27, and will be covered in depth in this book.

While we are blessed with the world's greatest and first written constitution, given as a gift from God through inspired men, it has been coupled with an inefficient, unjust and unrighteous system to elect our leaders. If we want better government, we need to be better people and elect better people to represent us. This is difficult under the current political system. If we fix this fatal flaw, we are well on our way to fixing the problem.

CONCEPT SUMMARY

The simple answer to America's problems and the key to unlocking an almost unfathomable future glory are found by returning to the concepts of freedom, independence, responsibility, liberty, peace, and justice. In order to take back America, the citizenry (you and I) will have to become just and responsible, peaceful and independent, free and at liberty.

The first principle of just representation is hope. This hope is centered on God and true eternal principles.

"And I will restore thy judges as at the first, and thy counselors as at the beginning: afterward thou shalt be called, The city of righteousness, the faithful city." (Isaiah 1:26)

President George Washington, our very first chief judge, was called to serve as opposed to campaigning for the position. This was according to Jefferson's model of just representation. This concept was lost with the usurpation that came from party politics, special interests, mob democracy, and money power.

The blessings of Heaven will accompany our return to the important concepts of correct government as at the first (Isaiah 1:26). This is the basis of the work suggested by this book. The first principle of just representation is hope. This hope is centered on God and the promises of the covenant.

CONCEPT NUMBER TWO
CALLING AND ELECTION

"...the whole head is sick...thy princes are rebellious and companions of thieves. Every one loveth gifts and followeth after rewards."

-Isaiah 1:5, 23

The power of the call to serve is the power to place statesmen above the promises, deception, and self-promotion of the politician.

A politician is someone who will promise all that he can in order to get what he wants. A statesman is someone who will give all that he can in order to achieve what is best.

Politicians lie. Statesmen serve. Each is the great antithesis of the other. This Earth is set up as a great battlefield where each of us as individuals chooses what type of system we will support. These choices have eternal consequences. The Kingdom of Hell is administered under the greatest politician of all eternity. He desperately seeks to establish his order on Earth, and for a time has been incredibly successful. Politically, the American playing field has been tilted heavily towards the politician.

The God of Heaven is the greatest statesman of all eternity. His love for a fallen world is so great that He sent His Son as a Redeemer to lift and bring the order of Heaven to Earth. The battle lines are drawn. The captains of each side are calling "come join the ranks." In any great battle the most dangerous place is always the middle ground. Trying to avoid conflict by hiding in the middle is putting yourself in a position of little use to either side. Yet the middle ground is exactly where great throngs of the foolish and uncommitted will seek to position themselves. The lukewarm, uncommitted fence-sitters will be the first to be judged and found unfit to enter the body of Christ. Their judgment is as sure as the word of God.

"I know thy works, that thou art neither cold nor hot: I would thou wert cold or hot. So then because thou art lukewarm, and neither cold nor hot, I will spue thee out of my mouth." (Revelation 3:15-16)

The call will be answered

In recent times, many Americans expect someone else to take responsibility for us. In essence, we tell the politician "You decide to run for political office, convince us that you are the person who will do the most for us and take care of us, then once elected don't bother us until next election." This system is destroying America. America is now calling you to serve. This call is issued according to the Biblical principle of calling the many, then a few (the best and most qualified) will be chosen (Matthew 22:14). The Independence Movement is about this call. The call will be answered because there is still much love in our country. We love our fellow man. This is the basis of justice. We love and respect ourselves and hold ourselves to the high standards that we should be able to expect from others, this is the basis responsibility.

The call to serve is more than just a religious concept.

In reality the call to serve is the basis of authority in both true religion and correct government. In religion a valid call to serve and represent God comes from Heaven downward. In government, a valid call to serve and represent the people comes from the people upward. In both cases, we qualify for the call by following Christ, who is our great example. The valid call and correct principles are essential to the proper functioning of both true religion and correct government.

There is real power in this call to serve. As people respond to the just representation of the Independence Movement, real beneficial change is not only possible, but inevitable. The beauty of the Independence Movement is that the necessary change and the elimination of the spoils system can be accomplished within the framework of an existing or a new political party or parties. The participants simply change the candidate nomination, campaigning, and party politicking procedures, and hold themselves to the higher standards of the Independence Movement.

We participate in the movement and cast our vote for those thus called to serve. If the voters choose to elect leaders called to serve by a superior, more representative, just and efficient movement, then we will have those leaders to serve us. We should never underestimate the power of good people working together. We thus harness the power and patriotism of America for good. It is foolish to continue doing what we have been doing and expect to get results other than what we have been getting. As we change for the better, we can expect things to change for the better.

How to avoid wolves in sheep's clothing

The present political system is designed to elect our representatives based on what they say. The Savior specifically commanded us that we shall "know them by their fruits." (Matthew 7:16, 20) The promise given that by so doing we would avoid "false prophets which come to you in sheep's clothing, but inwardly they are ravening wolves (Matthew 7:15).

Many fail to see the political relevance of this scripture because of their definition of "prophet". The greatest prophecies of the Biblical prophets are their promises to the people that if they lived in a prescribed manner, they will be blessed as people, families, communities, and nations. A politician is elected upon his promises of what the future will be if he is elected. This makes him a prophet. If those promises are based upon false pretexts, then inevitably they will become false promises or prophecies, and the politician a false prophet. The ravening wolf in sheep's clothing is a good description of the power-hungry politician. The infiltrated flock is in grave peril.

The basic foundation of our American system is threatened with destruction. Infiltration of the socialists from within and the threat of communism from without are threats very much alive today. The ten planks of the Communist Manifesto (discussed later in more detail) are openly preached by many of our nation's most powerful politicians. These same planks are a religion preached (at the exclusion of Christianity) five days a week to our children via the public education system. John Dewey, an ardent socialist, is considered the father of our modern public educational system.

Many are lulled to sleep by the purported death of communism. The Book of Revelation specifically warns the scarlet beast (communism) would only appear dead. This warning is repeated five times (Revelation 13:3; 13:12; 13:14; 17:8; 17:11).

The great false prophet, Karl Marx, could never stand the scrutiny of being judged by his fruits. Not only has his system been proven to be a hoax and a lie, but the man's life was one of squalor. Here was a man totally unable to take care of himself without the charity of others. His home was described as one of filth, confusion, and poverty. Yet in this irresponsible position he married and became a father. In 1862 Marx wrote, "Daily my wife tells me she wished she were lying in the grave with the children, and truly I cannot blame her."[4] Here is a man so selfishly caught up in himself that he literally left his own family starving while he sought the favors and attention of the idle rich. The pain and suffering of his own family has thus been perpetrated upon whole nations, and the hollowness of the man mimicked by the hollowness of a whole system.

Our Nation has been seduced

How could our nation, built upon the foundation of a basic belief in God, be so seduced by a system which, according to its authors, is specifically designed to "dethrone God"? We must repent of our red and scarlet sins. We begin this process by ceasing to make our judgments of politicians by what they say. Instead, we must begin to elect statesmen based upon the fruits of

---

[4] W. Cleon Skousen, *The Naked Communist*, Salt Lake City, Utah Reviewer 1958 pg. 350

their personal, family, public and private lives. Imagine all the pain and suffering the world could have avoided if Adolf Hitler had been judged by the fruits of his pre-political life instead of being brought to power by the force of his lies.

As long as we continue to support a system that elects politicians based upon what they say instead of what they are, we are in danger of losing all that we cherish most. We will have "wolves in sheep's clothing" for leaders as long as we continue to support a system that chooses leaders based upon what they say (Matthew 7:15-20).

Many argue that it doesn't matter what a person's personal life is like so long as he is able to "deliver the goods politically." How truly shallow a person must be to accept such words. What a true politician it would take to make such a statement. Talent is never enough. We must insist upon integrity, ideally coupled with talent. But, given a choice, integrity is much more important to the preservation of freedom and liberty than raw talent or ability. A man who is educated without morals may become simply a "clever devil". The greatest danger of deception comes when the worthy goal is coupled with evil intention. It is so easy for a trained deceiver to keep our attention upon the worthy goal through his speech, while the fraud of his evil intent is perpetrated upon us. Usually the cost of such a fraud is measured in terms of the loss of freedom and liberty, while the value of the worthy goal is minimized or eliminated through inefficient or misdirected centralized administration. To the politician though, results are never as important as to whom the credit eventually goes.

Daniel Webster said, "Good intention will always be pleaded for every assumption of power...It is hardly too strong to say that the Constitution was made to guard the people against the dangers of good intentions. There are men in all ages who mean to govern well, but they mean to govern. They promise to be good masters, but they mean to be masters."[5]

---

[5] Daniel Webster 1782-1852. Online quote from Quoteworld.org

We must realize that the greedy and the power hungry will gravitate to where they are most likely to be able to satisfy their lust. The American political system, as currently in use, is the "biggest game in town". When we make our decisions for leaders, only upon the basis of what they say, then people, whose works have been darkness from a life of taking, are still eligible to work the system for their own advantage.

Great American statesmen serve in spite of obstacles

How truly grateful we are for the many great American statesmen who have entered and remained in the fray of the political battlefield in spite of the ever increasing tilt of that field. If we allow this tilt to continue, the true statesman will soon be faced with a wall that will all but exclude the just and honorable from the system. The fact that current American politics are not fair is not new to anyone. In fact, the dirtiness of modern politics is so repugnant to most good people, few want to enter the field where they are needed most.

The statesman enters politics to protect that which is most valuable; personal freedom and liberty, and that of family, friends, and neighbors esteemed as brothers and sisters. Not being dishonest, he is loath to promise that which is not his to give. He will not curtail his own independence by indenturing himself to the many special interest groups who are more than willing to purchase favors. Since the true statesman correctly has his priorities as God first, family second, and country third, he has to balance his devotion and time given to each. So much of current politics center around the indignity and corruption associated with the need to constantly beg for money or the injustice of sacrifice of personal fortunes by those who serve. This must change.

If our system of government is allowed to become so complex and demanding that it requires the personal sacrifice of a statesman's family, fortune and soul, then ultimately, only those without family, fortune and soul will be left to serve. The politician without family values, dependent financially upon special interests, and left soulless in the process, may be a most dangerous place for us to place our trust. We need a system that shifts the burden to the shoulders of many citizen statesmen involved in a government that truly is theirs.

The focus of the statesman's life has been to give, to serve, to love, and to build. His work has been done in the light. We need a system that will fairly elect statesmen to represent us. There, they will continue to be honorable because it comes naturally to them (Luke 6:43-45). Is it fair to expect statesmen to enter politics if they are subjected to great injustices?

The great unfairness of the political party system is imposed as a burden upon the statesman striving to work for that which is best. The statesman may be forced to compromise, compete unfairly with the politicians, or even become a politician himself. The answer is not to reform a bad system but to replace it with a system of just representation; a system of equality and fairness based upon the protection of freedom and liberty. The good news is that such a system is possible. This system can call the best people to represent us and make it easier for them to serve and be effective.

God's hand is evident from the very beginning

The words "One Nation under God" have been our reality. We desperately need to re-discover our roots. The Prophet Isaiah speaks to us today,

> "Hear, O heavens, and give ear, O earth: for the Lord hath spoken, I have nourished and brought up children, and they have rebelled against me.
>
> "Ah sinful nation, a people laden with iniquity, a seed of evildoers, children that are corrupters: they have forsaken the Lord, they have provoked the Holy One of Israel unto anger, they are gone away backward."
> (Isaiah 1:2-4)

John the Revelator's description of the coming peace is possible because the "Devil and Satan" is bound a thousand years. The effect being that he is "shut up", that he should **deceive the nations** no more (Revelation 20:2, 3). Notice that the devil is politically active. The devil can be bound and shut up by people finally becoming wise enough to cease to listen to his voice. A first step in the process is to see that evil people do not gain the control and power they seek through government, regardless of what may be promised. This can be accomplished by electing only the most honorable people to represent us.

Learning about righteousness by observing God's works
The Father of our spirits reaches down to us with two Godly attributes, the balance of which is defined as righteousness. The first attribute is justice and the second is mercy. A person whose Godly life is exemplified by justice and mercy treats others the way he would like to be treated, (justice defined) and uses his power, strength, and ability to lift others (mercy defined). This is how we judge a good candidate for the responsibilities of government.

America's greatness has been, and always will be, a product of its goodness. God plainly identifies our problem. "Oh my people, they which lead thee cause thee to err, and destroy the way of thy paths" (Isaiah 3:12). As prophesied, our nation will return to being one nation under God. The question is, will that return be before or after we feel the chastening hand of a jealous and forgotten God.

The call to serve is sanctioned by God
Imagine the call to serve answered by many people, each person willing to becoming a candidate within a great political movement. Imagine a people who know what the oath of office means and are each willing to live it and answer the call. Imagine an efficient system to issue the call to serve and represent at the neighborhood level with an effective system for responsibility to go up, and accountability to come down to each individual who cares enough to become involved. It has been stated that as far as getting things done in politics, that work done

at the organizing level is a thousand times as effective as work accomplished later, including voting on election day. Imagine a system that focuses on effective organization to put the best man ahead of party politics, special interests, mob democracy, and money power, to go before the voters with the confidence of a call to serve and the backing of extensive citizen support. Imagine people, organized, committed, and working together to make it happen. This is the Independence Movement. It all starts with the call to serve. We answer the call individually, help issue the call publicly, and work together to make the call meaningful.

The difference that makes all the difference

The call to serve is the little change that can change everything. The call to serve is power. If we are to become a nation of kings and priests unto God (Revelation 1:6) then the power of the call is crucial. A priest unto God is a call to serve and represent God. The call comes from Heaven downward. This is the foundation of true religion. A political call is a call to serve and represent the people. This call comes from the people upward. This is the foundation of correct government. The reality of the American system is that it should be all about this call, but it has been usurped by party politics, special interests, mob democracy, and money power. These will remain enthroned until something more powerful replaces them. The call to serve is just such a power.

The following model is offered to help understand who we are as kings and priests under God, how we relate to Him, the importance of any call to serve, and the balance of many principles. We can use this model to easily teach these principles to our children and others.

Much of this model is of ancient date. You will recognize other parts as used earlier in this book. It was a wonderful revelation to see it all fit together.

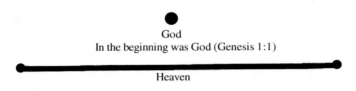

God

In the beginning was God (Genesis 1:1)

Heaven

(Two planes of existance were created. One was
set for man to reach up towards, and one was set
as a foundational support for man to stand upon.)

Earth

God is a righteous being with the love of an eternal
Father. His righteousness is the balance of two great extensions
of his love, by which he reaches down to lift man. The first is
justice, which empowers the order of Heaven. The second is
mercy (the use of his power to lift and bless) which enables
agency. This power extends all the way to this Earth as long as
man looks towards the source of this power. This becomes
symbolic of a mountain that, with effort, can be climbed to reach
the Lord. The higher we climb the greater our perspective and
the closer we are to Heaven.

**Agency and order, on the Heavenly plane under God, are
two great ideals held in balance by universal love.**

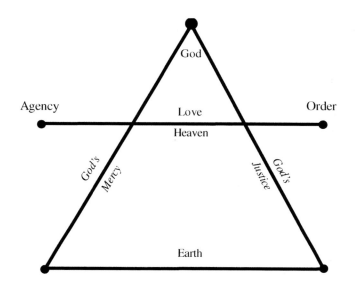

On the agency side we have freedom (lack of oppression) which is possible because of independence, which comes because of the acceptance of responsibility. On the order side we have liberty (the ability to move and act in a society). In order for there to be liberty, there must be peace. Peace is possible in a society only as the people live in justice, which means that they treat others the way they themselves want to be treated.

Love is the power that exalts God as the eternal sovereign

Love is also the power that raises man to a position of individual sovereignty. As we love our fellow man, the liberty of society is secure upon the peace of a people living justly. Love also preserves that which is most precious for our self. Love of self causes us to seek, obtain and maintain our freedom through independence. This comes from accepting the responsibilities upon which the independence is based.

The Heavenly love of God is abundantly manifested in the actions of His Son, our King and High Priest called of God to Earth. Heaven reaches down to the Earthly plane with revelation and redemption. Revelation comes to the Earth from Heaven through Christ who is the light of the world. Redemption comes as man accepts the King of Heaven as the ultimate King on Earth, and thus accepts the order of Heaven.

Whenever man stands in a position of Earthly government authority, he should realize that he stands in proxy for the Heavenly King, and act accordingly

In ancient Israel the authority and honor resided in the judgment seat and not in the individual temporarily occupying it. This reminded both official and citizen of the government's proper role. Elected representatives who humbly put aside self-interest become a chain in the redemption of the Earth. This then is then just a short step to the acceptance of Christ on Earth. We see that we have created a balanced star. The star has six points and seven enclosed spaces. Let's look now at each enclosed space and the significant representation created.

On the top we have a triangle with God at its apex over Heaven on a foundation of love. Reaching downward is God's justice and mercy. This is a good representation of the spiritual reality of God

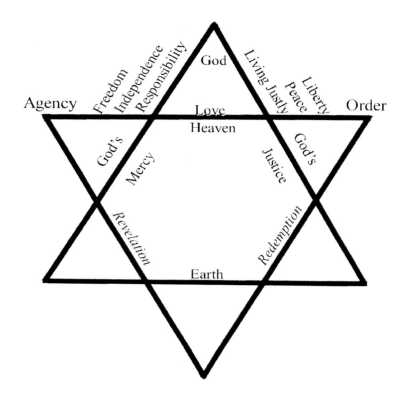

On the Left upper side is a triangle representing the church. Its three sides define true religion. The church is connected with the divine and thus touches Heaven. The church is a tool for God to extend His mercy. Revelation from Heaven defines its border. The call to serve (and thus represent God) is a form of this revelation.

On the right side we have a representation of the Kingdom of God. We see that correct government also touches Heaven. The redemption comes as the people, looking up, accept the King of Heaven as the ultimate King on Earth. This enables the justice on Earth to be the justice of God. This representation illustrates that the proper role of government is to assure justice. If government takes over the roll of administering mercy, justice will suffer.   Likewise if the church assumes the role of administering justice, its ability to administer mercy will be diminished.

A balanced individual holds to both justice and mercy
We should be involved to support both great works and be involved in both religion (administering mercy) and government (administering justice).   We stand upon the physical earth, thus illustrating the need to have support and take care of our physical needs in order to be able to stand and reach towards the heavens. A man so balanced will be able to touch Heaven and directly feel of God's love.   He will also enjoy the blessings of individual sovereignty, and use his power to lift and bless others.

The lower right and left triangles represent worldly religion and worldly government. The worldly plane means that lower forms of revelation (God's word mixed with the philosophies of men) and lower forms of justice are administered. The mercy and redemption are also lesser.   Worldly religion and government do have direct lines that can be climbed to reach the higher ideal, but if their draw is too strong, the individual will be pulled in a way that causes him to lose touch with Heaven.   This is where the individual is taught to let someone else take care of their religion or governing, the basis of individual sovereignty.

Last; we must understand what is lurking beneath. Below the physical plane created by God is a fallen being. He is not a creator, yet he would have it all funnel towards himself.

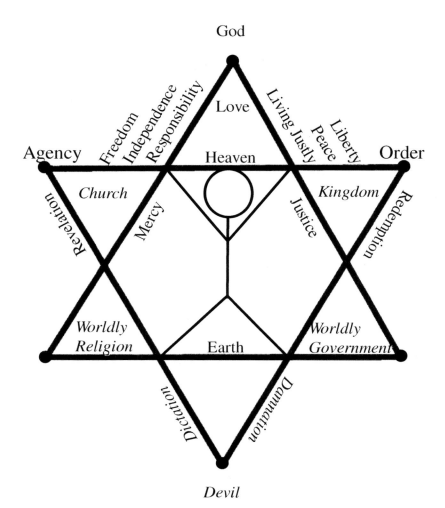

God

Love

Heaven

Agency

Freedom
Independence
Responsibility

Living Justly
Peace
Liberty

Order

Church

Revelation

Mercy

Justice

Kingdom

Redemption

Worldly
Religion

Earth

Worldly
Government

Dictation

Damnation

Devil

The imagery of the bottomless pit applies. The Devil was cast out of heaven because he was neither just nor merciful. In fact, he sought to destroy both God's justice and mercy by exalting himself. Where God would reveal to men what he should do, this being would be a dictator telling men what he must do. Instead of redemption to lift man to individual sovereignty, he would damn mankind, holding him down in dependency and control. This being has his Earthly followers and desperately seeks to see his order established on Earth. This being was cast to this Earth (Revelation 12:9) so we could experience opposition and have choice, thus giving agency to man. We choose where we will spend eternity by whom we choose to follow here on Earth.

Note: part of his model is original with the author and was used earlier in this book. This was incorporated with a Star of David model taken from an Encyclopedia Britannica. Later I tried to relocate this reference but was unsuccessful. After these two models came together, it was clear that the enclosed parts and the points of the model also were significant and they were easily labeled.

CONCEPT SUMMARY

Our current political system, fueled by party politics, special interests, mob democracy, and money power, favors the election of those who will promise the most. If we are to elect just representation, we must have the ability to go deeper than mere promises, and look for correct principle and good men to represent us. The second principle of just representation is the calling and election of righteous, just, honorable, and wise people to represent us. This is the means of being served by statesman instead of politicians.

CONCEPT NUMBER THREE
RIGHTS AND RESPONSIBILITIES

"Now therefore, if ye will obey my voice indeed, and keep my covenant, then ye shall be a peculiar treasure unto me above all people: for all the earth is mine:

"And ye shall be unto me a kingdom of priests, and an holy nation."   -Exodus 19:5-6

All rights and personal freedoms are gifts from God
These gifts, however, are conditional upon the acceptance of the responsibilities associated with each right. The acceptance of responsibility brings the independence that makes the rights of freedom possible. In the short run (in God's time, the very short run) it may seem to man that it is possible to cheat and selfishly acquire rights and freedoms at the expense of others. This is merely sin's illusion. A good measure of intelligence is the ability of an individual to grasp this concept. A society (or family) that shields the individual from the natural consequences of his or her actions, or gives mature individual's rights without responsibilities, is not only destroying the learning process of the individual, but ultimately the injustice destroys the peace of the society. Liberty within a society is based upon peace.

The only way for someone to acquire a right that they did not earn is for someone else to work for a right that they did not acquire. If done voluntarily in a way that lifts the individual we may call this mercy. If it is taken involuntarily in a way ultimately destructive to the taker we call this plunder. **All systems of injustice must have plunder to survive.** The quickest way to stop a system of injustice is to curtail the plundering. A family, nation, or even a world without peace can trace this to the violation of the natural laws upon which peace is based.

To some it may appear possible to break the eternal laws of justice that religious people call commandments. In reality, the sale price of sin is always the loss of personal freedom. "The fiddler is always paid". An institutionalized system of injustice may delay the inevitable, but payment will come, most often with exorbitant interest. If we want to give peace a chance, then we must give justice a chance. There is no peace for the unjust.

The acceptance of responsibilities brings independence

This is the basis of personal freedom. If we accept responsibilities not resulting in independence and freedom it is because we are accepting responsibilities that do not belong to us or we are participating in a system of plunder. Responsibility for others can be either plunder or mercy. Plunder destroys, mercy lifts. The most damaging plunder is plunder of personal independence by taking rights and responsibilities necessary for the individual to grow, progress, and pursue happiness. Many who accept plundered wealth via the socialist state are actually plundered most severely in that they personally lose their independence and rights which come from the acceptance of responsibilities.

It is God's justice that wonderful rewards of independence and freedom are ultimately given to the merciful (those who use their power, ability and earned rights to lift and bless others). "Blessed are the merciful for they shall obtain mercy" (Matthew 5:7). If we accept or take the responsibilities of others in ways that do not lift and bless, the effort is wasted. The destruction to the souls of those held in dependency and control may be eternal.

All rights can be traced to responsibilities
All responsibilities lead to natural rights

At times we enjoy rights that were earned by someone else (someone or God's mercy) but every right has to be earned. This is the basis of natural law. In order to comprehend the inseparability of rights and responsibilities under natural or eternal law, let's look at them together. We will begin by looking at the most famous of all responsibilities, the Ten

51

Commandments. When we call a responsibility a commandment and a right, a blessing, it is another way of acknowledging the hand of God in all things.

The first responsibility (commandment)
is to have no other gods before God

To the spiritually naive or intellectually lazy, this first commandment may seem like angry words from an egotistical or selfish being. When looked at with the faith of a child and in terms of the blessings and the rights stemming from this, the greatest of all commandments, we clearly see why God in His great love made this commandment first. The blessings of order and agency from which hang society's liberty and the individual's freedom are secure only upon the basis of the recognition of God first. To clearly illustrate this point lets look at this commandment in terms of a family relationship.

God is reverently referred to as Father for a reason

Imagine a father who gathered his large family together and said "From now on I will no longer assume the responsibilities of the head of this household. Because I will no longer be responsible, there are no longer any responsibilities required of you. You are now completely free to use this home that I have built and all the resources of this household any way you see fit. You older and bigger children can now take whatever you can and use it any way you wish. You smaller and weaker children find someone else to be your example and protector."

There are no longer any household rules so everyone is completely free, right? No rules, no laws, no order, no responsibility, yet the consequences of power in the hands of the mentally, spiritually, emotionally, or intellectually immature, may be shocking. We imagine a horrible scene of destruction and abuse. The rampant and wanton destruction and abuse so prevalent in this world is the direct result of God's spiritual children abandoning their father and not visa-versa.

Children can choose to live outside of the protection and order of God's household. This is also evidence of His love

While a very high value is placed upon order, an equally high value is placed upon agency. God is interested in seeing His children "grow up". This growing up is measured in terms of His children developing the ability to love. Order can be enforced at the expense of agency, or agency can be unbridled at the expense of order, but if they both are to be achieved in balance, there must be love. Love cannot be forced.

When we put no other gods before the Father, we experience an outpouring of God's love. We feel His unconditional love for us as individuals. God is always there for us. God's willingness to listen, His belief and faith in us, and the way His love lifts us is proof of that love. When we respond to this great and eternal love, we find that God helps us grow by letting us experience the joy that comes through the assumption of greater responsibilities. This brings even greater rights and freedoms. These greater responsibilities usually come to us in the form of opportunities to lift and bless others the very same way that God lifts and blesses us. This is the process of establishing the kingdom of God on Earth with both order and agency balanced by love.

The rights associated with no other gods before God are the blessings of agency and order

All the pain and suffering caused by the abuses of agency and order can be directly associated with rejection of responsibilities of the first commandment. The order of Heaven is based on order. There are consequences for the destruction of the order. This is the justice of God and is also a manifestation of His love.

Could it be that part of the order of Heaven is that even the great God of Heaven rules by the consent of the governed? Judging by the actions of His Son, our Redeemer, into whose hand was committed the Father's power; we see that He could not be tempted to use that power to rule over any except those who voluntarily offered their heart and labor in love. In fact, we learn a great lesson about the nature of temptation from the temptations of Christ. What the Devil offered were the very rights that were to be the Son of Man's. The offer was made before Christ had taken the responsibilities associated with those rights including responsibility for our sins. The responsibility must always come first in God's order.

Rejection of responsibility is a rejection of God

Responsibilities lead to rights under God. Irresponsibility leads to the loss of rights. All rights ultimately come from God because God grants agency unto man. God has the ability to oppress man, because He is governed by His own love, He chooses not to do so. Choosing to accept responsibility brings independence and makes freedom possible. This is the essence of having no other gods before Him. The great evil act is taking someone's freedom. One way this is done is by destroying the independence by removing the God-given right to take responsibility.

When religion is used to dominate, control, and destroy liberty and freedom, we can judge who its author is. This false religion is less than worthless. We must allow freedom of conscience, but the acts of lawbreakers should never be tolerated, especially if done in the name of religion. When leaders practice false religion within any organization, it becomes the responsibility of the flock to cleanse first, that which is within their own organization (Matthew 23:26).

One of the saddest times in all of Biblical history was the rejection of the responsibilities of self-rule and independence. This was when the Children of Israel requested a king.

"But the thing displeased Samuel, when they said, Give us a king to judge us. And Samuel prayed unto the Lord.

"And the Lord said unto Samuel, Hearken unto the voice of the people in all that they say unto thee: for they have not rejected thee, but they have rejected me, that I should not reign over them."   (1 Samuel 8:6-7)

This act was not a total rejection of God because the people came to God's prophet and requested the king be appointed under God's direction. If we ever elect a leader who is allowed to assume the dictatorial power of a king simply because the man wants the power, it will be a total rejection of God. There are degrees of this rejection. As a nation, we are far from guiltless.

A nation that has no other gods before the true God of Heaven is a nation sublimely blessed with liberty, freedom, peace, independence, justice, and responsibility.   The commandment to put God first means that we recognize that there is nothing else of sufficient value to trade for these rights.

Jefferson's personal motto
When we come to this understanding, we also understand the great and true principle that resistance to tyranny is service to God. This was said so well by Jefferson's personal motto, "I have sworn upon the altar of almighty God, eternal hostility against every form of tyranny over the mind of man." Responsibility to resist tyranny led to the American Revolution. An equal truth is that the acceptance of tyranny is a rejection of God. A people who have rejected God have little claim upon His guidance, protection, and deliverance. The free man can turn out tyranny with much less effort compared to the slave who has another man as a master. The slave can scarcely lift up his head to the slightest level of dignity without great peril.

God places great importance upon responsibility to reject tyranny. If people are united in rejection of tyranny, tyranny will always be fractionated and impotent. Individuals or small groups of unjust people by themselves have limited success to aggrandize themselves or appease their petty lust for power. If people become united to accept a system of tyranny, the tyranny will also become united. Every unjust man seeking power will gravitate towards the centralized control in lock-stepped unity to divide the plundered spoils and deliver the enforced oppression. This is how Hell enlarges its boundaries beyond the borders of the bottomless pit.

Tyranny has a great weakness and soft underbelly

A system that needs plunder to survive (a definition of tyranny) can only survive as long as the cost of the plundering is less than the value of the plunder. We have a responsibility to see that what we have produced and created is not used for evil purposes. It is very difficult to enslave those whose love and allegiance to God is greater than even love of their own life. This is the formula that won the war in Heaven fought against the Dragon and his angels.

"And they overcame him by the blood of the Lamb, and by the word of their testimony; and they loved not their lives unto the death." (Revelation 12:11)

Thomas Paine, patriot, put it this way:

"These are the times that try men's souls. The summer soldier and the sunshine patriot will, in this crisis, shrink from the service of their country; but he that stands it now deserves the love and thanks of man and woman. Tyranny, like Hell, is not easily conquered; yet we have this consolation with us, that the harder the conflict, the more glorious the triumph. What we obtain too cheaply, we esteem too lightly; it is dearness only that gives every thing its value. Heaven knows how to put a proper price upon its goods; and it would be strange indeed if so celestial an article as Freedom should not be highly rated."[6]

---

[6] Patrick Henry, *American Liberty Virginia Convention of Delegates.* March 23rd, 1775

The second responsibility (commandment)

Not make unto thee any graven image is closely related to the first responsibility and is a specific commandment against idolatry. The commandments of God were engraved upon stone. This commandment specifically removes confusion about God and the origins of His commandments by removing man made competition. The rights associated with this commandment are those already mentioned.

The third responsibility (commandment)

Not taking the name of God in vain is given for the same reason as the previous commandments. If the name of Deity is reduced to common cussing, how difficult is it to then use the same words in reverent worship or confident supplication in time of need? While the person who vainly uses God's name in base language is making a personal choice to reject God, the damage to the culture of a society can be immeasurable as the rising generation is denied reverence and respect for themselves and the being in whose image they were created. The misuse of God's name is a disgrace to God's family. This is not a victimless transgression. The greater responsibility of this commandment is to see that the name of Deity is not used as an endorsement or excuse to abuse freedom, destroy liberty, or support tyranny and plunder. The amount of eternal truth in a religion compared to the inroads made by the philosophies of men is evaluated by the bench-marks of freedom and liberty. The Lord will not hold guiltless he who uses the name of Deity to promote the doctrines of the devil.

The standards of our society and laws of our land protect the individual against his name being used for slander, defamation, or illegal promotion of another's self-interest, without license. Some people are correctly adamant about protecting individuals from being hatefully maligned, yet feel any sacrilege against Deity is a guaranteed right. Would we approve of our name becoming a cuss word? Common courtesy, respect, and decency, should to be enough to assure compliance with this responsibility. Shakespeare put it this way, "He who filches from me my good name robs me of that which not enriches him, and make me poor indeed".[7] It makes little sense to do something that offends just for the sake of being offensive.

The remaining responsibilities (commandments) are the basis of self-rule

These commandments assure justice, peace, and liberty within one's self, family, community, and nation. They are a natural extension of loving oneself and others. We extend the standard of how one desires to be treated, towards others. The morally advanced, intelligent, and experienced person will govern himself by love. He is intelligent enough to realize in advance the rights (blessings) associated with living justly and the loss to oneself and society associated with injustice.

Responsibilities associated with keeping the Sabbath day holy bring the rights or blessings of individuals trained in the principles of eternal law

Time is reserved to receive Heaven's mercy and the joy associated with extending that mercy to others. The Sabbath is a special day of service to God, profound rest, and reflection centered on family, and the realization that in the eternal sense, we all are one family under God. The holiness of the day is built around worship. The best English word to describe worship is emulation. As we strive to become like God through worship, we acquire His attributes. These are the very attributes that bring freedom to the individual and liberty to society. The New Testament teaching that the Sabbath was made for man and not visa-versa is a recognition of the tremendous blessing this day can bring.

The responsibility of honoring father and mother begins with the recognition that the Kingdom of God is first established in

---

[7] William Shakespeare, *Othello III*, Act III, 155, England 1605.

one's heart. This next extends to the family

There is a responsibility for parents to be honorable and to treat their physical offspring in the same way that God treats us as spiritual offspring. Children learn about God's mercy and justice by observing these principles in the home. If parents are not honorable, children will still be abundantly blessed by honoring what they "should be" and reestablishing that order, in time, within their own home. This is the way to honor parents even if they are not honorable. This is the great foundation of society's peace. The promise from God, that thy days may be long upon the land which the Lord thy God giveth thee, are the blessings of peace. Peace is the basis for the longevity within one's self, family, community, and nation. A society torn apart by injustice will be short-lived. This is true whether one lives with alone, as husband and wife, in a family, community, or nation.

Responsibilities to not murder, steal, commit adultery, or bear false witness, are the responsibilities to respect the sovereignty of other individuals within society

This is the basis of our own rights to be reciprocally treated equally under the laws of justice. Rights are protected under the authority of self-defense delegated to the government by the people.

The last responsibility to not covet is the basis of equality

Recognize that property, wealth, and relationships are an expression of life and liberty coupled with expended individual energy. Desiring rights without work or responsibilities is a good definition of coveting. Confusion about equality comes when we think of equality only in terms of possessions. Since possessions are the result of work, and the end result of work is an expression of individuality, to force the equality of possessions destroys the individuality and sovereignty of the persons within a society.

Individuality is the basis of all rights. We should be absolutely just and equal in protecting rights to pursue happiness with security of life and liberty. Effort to force equalization of possessions destroys equalization of basic rights to use individuality and life to pursue happiness. All efforts to equalize property by force are driven by either covetness, or ignorance. A politician may covet the unearned rights of power. The ignorant and lazy covet the rights associated with the labor of others.

We have slipped so far down the path of socialism that few now question the morality of un-rightful taking

It now seems perfectly all right for a politician to brazenly go before a special interest group and promise to use the government force, or police power, to rob and plunder another group to provide direct benefits to this group. Cheers and applause usually follows. This injustice destroys peace. Power, intimidation, and control, must be used to make someone else give up what is coveted. The socialist politician (false prophet) walks the slippery path of trying to keep the peace by promising everything to everyone and getting all to buy into the basic immorality of the system. The propaganda of the socialized press has been very effective in speeding this degenerative process. The peace becomes increasingly difficult to keep as the society becomes less productive and the lust for plunder increases. If the immorality of injustice continues to escalate, eventually it will be necessary to either kill or enslave those who do not wish to be plundered. If the power to kill or enslave unjustly is tolerated, then the power of the police state, with all of its appendages, becomes necessary. That which is most precious, individual sovereignty, the rights and blessings of self-rule, and the future happiness of posterity, is traded for a mess of pottage and Hell on Earth. We would then become subjects to evil. It could (and would) get worse as we continue to descend into the bottomless pit.

If a system of plunder is allowed to perpetuate itself, every individual within that society will eventually face their own turn at being plundered.

This is not a matter of if, but only when. How we protect the rights of others is the standard by which we are judged. This occurs most often as a consequence of natural law, here and now. Certainly the eternal consequences can be escaped by none. The man without guile is free of covetness. He sees every individual in equality with respect for individual sovereignty. Those who see the individual in terms of possessions are easily deceived into destroying the great basis of equality, which is the equality of rights. The actual work of destruction is always driven by enmity and greed, the essence of covetness. Look beyond rhetorical lies of the communists and socialists and see the foundation of the system is based on covetness. To the communist and socialist, the life and property of others has always been cheap when compared to the dearness of their own. When we finally see this, the actual behavior of the Marxist robber is no longer a mystery.

In a society based upon the just concept of private ownership of property, it is possible for people to learn to give, to be generous, to sacrifice, and enjoy the blessings of responsibility, independence, and freedom. While it is evil and wrong to force an equalization of property, there is a higher order of equalization. This order is based upon the fullest respect for individual sovereignty. When a person fully acknowledges that all blessings flow from above, then it becomes natural to consecrate and regard the blessings as belonging to God. Wonderful freedom is then experienced as a person no longer worries about his "stuff." We let God watch over what is his. We simply live in a manner to thankfully accept every blessing and use the resources before us to do as much good as possible. This giving of oneself fully to God is a prelude to the promise of receiving an inheritance of "all things" (Revelation 21:7). We trade our all for His, which turns out to be a very good trade, even here and now. There is no greater equalization than this.

As stated in the first of this book, the purpose of true

religion is to teach correct principles. We then govern ourselves and use agency to lift ourselves and others. The purpose of true government is to protect rights so we can practice true religion.

The Devil and followers want more than anything else to be worshiped.

This is not for what they can give, but for what they can take. This is why they put themselves between man and the blessings of Heaven. These blessings are the natural outpouring from personal acceptance of responsibility. Destroy the responsibility and you destroy the right. Disassociate the reward with the effort to produce it and instill confusion about who provided the natural resources used in the creation of the wealth and "Walla! Smoke and mirrors," it appears that government is the source of the blessing. A new god has been created. We have man worshiping man. Since the Devil is the fountain of this greed, lust, hate, envy, and covetness, he becomes the god of this world. This temporary or temporal state of affairs is allowed so that man may learn by his own experience the difference between good and evil and the justice of God upon the Devil and his followers can be carried out. This is the essence of the battle of good against evil.

This same method of evaluating the Ten Commandments can be used to see the value to the individual in terms of rights, (blessings), and responsibilities (commandments) given by God to man.

CONCEPT SUMMARY

Rights and responsibilities are inseparably connected. The third principle of just representation is the protection of rights and responsibility accomplished through limited government. Government must be wise and restrained enough to take neither right nor responsibility from the people served, except those proper roles specifically delegated to it by just law.

CONCEPT NUMBER FOUR
THE POWER OF LOVE VS.
THE LOVE OF POWER

"No servant can serve two masters: for either he will hate the one, and love the other; or else he will hold to the one, and despise the other. Ye cannot serve God and mammon."
-Luke, 16:13

Two systems of government are competing for acceptance in America today

Limited government is based upon individual responsibility and rights and is driven by the power of love. Unlimited government, based upon dependency and control, is driven by the love of power. Limited government protects equality of rights and opportunity. Unlimited government serves the assumption of the superiority of a ruling class over everyone else, thus an assumed natural right to lead, and an unconditional responsibility for the rest to follow. Limited government promises nothing, yet has delivered the highest standard of living the world has ever known. Unlimited government promises everything, yet has consistently delivered the closest thing to Hell on Earth the world has ever known.

The power of love is the greatest power in the universe.

Love lifts, it builds, it inspires, it is patient, it teaches, it enlightens, it conquers all. Love also has its counterfeits. One of these is the great Whore Babylon (Revelation chapters 17 and 18). When she stands naked in the light of day she will have lost all of her appeal. She will be seen for what she is, the great controller, old, worn, and her body covered with putrefying sores. Every act of injustice has left its ugly mark. What has appeared to be beauty under the cover of darkness will be seen as nothing more than the thickest paint and shadowy illusion. The great lie can never stand the bright light.

While scoffers huddle in despair to feed each other on

intellectual cynicism, great patriots awake to rebuild, repair, polish, and take out the trash around the beautiful, but neglected, temple that is the United States Constitution. The scoffers and shirkers at the time of the American Revolution denied themselves the opportunity to associate with the greatest movement in the history of the world. The glory of what could have been theirs was forever lost. What would they trade now for one chance to go back and be a part of that great and rising glory? Now is our turn. The restoration of our Republic is our nation's future. If we fail to take our part in this great work, generations of posterity yet unborn will feel the shame of our inaction. Eternal glory and gratitude will forever follow the great ones whose work in saving the Republic will place their names emblazoned in glory along side those of our nation's founders. We are certain of a Heavenly reward extended to the great thinkers, builders, pioneers, workers, and fighters of our nation's birth. How will we face them if we cannot with confidence lift our eyes and say yes, we also loved and served the cause of freedom and liberty?

The words of Patrick Henry ring in our ears:

"Why stand we here idle? What is it that gentlemen wish? What would they have? Is life so dear, or peace so sweet, as to be purchased at the price of chains and slavery? Forbid it, Almighty God! I know not what course others may take; but as for me, give me liberty, or give me death!"[8]

The Constitution is the law of the land. We must throw the law breakers out to restore the goodness that is the strength of America. The light on the hill has not gone out. How thankful we are to the authors of our constitutional form of government. We are legally guaranteed the right to accomplish this restoration by peaceful means.

---

[8] Thomas Payne, *American Crisis*, December 1776

Restoring righteous judges in place of politicians

When we say that we are going to restore righteous judges in the place of politicians, the scoffers will say, "I hope you have a lot of money, because it takes a lot of money to be in politics today". We answer that a system that is run by money can be controlled by money. We intend to establish a system in which money does not have a vote and thus restore the vote to the people where it belongs.

The scoffers say "our enemies are too well established". We say the Constitution is established. We say the enemies of the Constitution occupy only the tenuous position of squatters and usurpers.

The scoffers will say "they have the media". We say our story will be told and retold a thousand times a million and the power of the message will be carried to the very hearts and souls of a sleeping nation.

The scoffers will say "nobody cares". We say that I care and you care, and that is enough to go to work. We care not what others may say, "as for me and my household, we will serve the Lord." (Joshua 24:15)

The scoffers will say "they are too many". We say that they that be for us are more than they that be against us. Our eyes have been opened (2 Kings 6:16-17).

The scoffers will say "it is foolish to try". We say that all that is necessary for our success the great God of Heaven has placed within our grasp. When we begin to exercise faith and make use of what we do have, instead of looking for excuses to shirk our responsibility, then what God wants to happen will happen and it will be miraculous.

The scoffers will say "their power is great". We say that our trust is in the Great Power.

God's success formula

There is a success formula with power to transform the world, or any organization, endeavor, project, or person. This is the first recorded divine instructions given to man. God's work and glory, like that of any good father is to lift and bless His children. After God revealed the work accomplished in the creation for our benefit, and before turning over this family business to his children, man was commanded to be fruitful, multiply, and replenish.

Be fruitful, to begin with a faith in the divine law of the harvest. **Multiply;** to take what we have and improve and increase upon it. We are also told to **replenish,** to put back more than we take. The third part insures the ability to sustain the work. If we take more than we put back, any living object (including relationships) will eventually die. Sin is death. The responsibility to replenish precedes the rights of dominion. People filled with love approach life this way. When this type of love is applied to saving our country, we will see a return of paradise. There is a natural multiplying of this effect in society as good people doing good things become its foundation.

The power is to be in the people

If people begin to believe the goodness of society comes from government, then the power will be shifted to the government. Order will then begin to crush agency. The proper role of government is not to do the good, but rather to allow the good to receive free and proper expression. The real power is to be in the people. This is the pursuit of happiness. The goodness from God, coupled with a worshiping or following on Earth, brings redemption to the Earth.

An evil trick to cheat the people out of their birthright is to try to remove God from the picture. Once accomplished it becomes easy to foster the belief that whoever controls any resource owns it and is thus justified in making all pay for its use. The Earth's resources rightly belong to God to be used by agency (permission) for the benefit of his children. Man only owns improvements made by his own work and creativity. The teachings of Christianity tell us how to give and put back of what we have so freely received. Millions of people effecting change in millions upon millions of ways, this is the power of the redemption. There must be freedom and liberty for this change to find full expression. A spark of the divine, fueled by love, will inspire each individual to seek out their own special opportunities to effect the greatest multiplying for good. What a beautiful thing it is to see someone filled with love give their own special gift to the world. We can see this art in every field, every type of work or endeavor, every service, charity, or creation of beauty. This is expressed in the following poem.

Grandpa's Garden
By Farley Anderson
Memories flood of long, long ago
When as a very little man,
I loved to be with Grandpa.
I was his biggest fan.
His garden was a special place,
For love and growth was there.
The flowers seemed as tall as trees
And made the people stare.
The rows were straight. The earth was warm,
And not a weed was seen.
The peas were sweet, the carrots long
A boy felt like a king

It didn't make much sense to me
How much he always grew,
For when I looked in his small house
All I could see was two.
Then every fall like old St. Nick,
A smile upon his face,
I saw my Grandpa sneak around
And fresh vegetablize the place.

The greatest mystery to me
Were the flowers that he grew.

68

You could not even eat them.
Their stems you could not chew.
I asked about this mystery,
The labor down the drain,
And so he paused to teach me
And my little brain.
"You see this world is vast and large.
I cannot change it all,
But this brown earth is my own space.
It is my special call."

"I make it like a paradise
For those who pass to see
What love, labor, toil and sweat
Can make this earth to be,
And when they smell this fragrance,
Their mind will upward turn
Problems lift, their heart will change.
For higher things they'll yearn.
I cannot make these flowers,
But I will do my share,
And God and I work side by side
To give them needed care."
One last thing he told me,
Though to learn it I was slow,
"For every flower you give away,
Two in its place will grow."
When from this life I travel
To that Garden eternally
And meet the master Gardner,
A welcomed child to be.
I will not be a stranger,
For I knew him here below,
And was taught about eternal things
While Grandpa leaned
Upon his hoe.

The Independence Movement is driven by the power of love

To maintain the goodness of freedom and liberty each person as an individual sovereign (king) works towards becoming a statesman to actively participate in government. The government then serves the people. When people are governed by the power of love, little or limited external government is needed. Sovereignty is held by God, and He gives sovereignty, rights, and power, to the people. This allows the fullest expression of good. Big, powerful, or unlimited government takes power, sovereignty, and rights from the people. The good then is only accomplished in a limited, second-hand way through the government, and not directly and more effectively by individuals. More power, rights and responsibilities to government is less power, rights, and responsibilities for the people under God.

The Independence Movement is driven by the power of love. We love truth enough to seek after the great truths. We love ourselves enough to settle for nothing less than our individual sovereignty. We love God enough to seek His order and do the works that will begin to establish that order on Earth. We love our children enough to humbly take them aside and apologize that we have allowed them to be taught the doctrines of covetness and control. We must love our children enough to teach them about heroes and great causes, about love and service, about the Heavenly banner of the Constitution and about the rights and responsibilities that make a nation great. We love our fellow men enough to see that the justice we seek for ourselves is justice for all. If we have enough love what can possibly stand in our way?

It was love that brought forth the miracle of Philadelphia, our Constitution. James Madison, known as the Father of the Constitution, said, "...every word of the constitution decides a question between power and liberty".[9] The Constitution is not a

---

[9] In addition to *America's Providential History* (noted above) another favorite book to introduce an inspirational view of American history *is Our Heritage of Freedom*, by D.P.Stoker and B.E. Clegg , 1998 Idaho Falls, Idaho

nebulous and difficult to understand document. Most confusion is the result of those who want power, seeking to justify their actions in light of a limiting contract they are sworn to uphold, and that is very specific in limiting their actions. The Constitution is not as much confusing as it is ignored.

Illustrating the Constitution's simplistic beauty

Let's consider a brief overview of the document. There are only seven (that's right, just seven) articles in the Constitution. The purpose of the Constitution was to establish a federal government of sufficient vitality to carry on the limited but necessary functions of a central government. Specifically and most importantly, the founders desired to limit that government to those functions and to keep the central government from growing to a point that it could oppress the people.

The first three articles of the constitution establish a system of checks and balances by dividing the functions of government into three separate branches; the Legislative, Executive, and Judicial. The two most important checks on the power of the central government, which were sovereignty of the individual and the established rights of the states, were already presumed.

The fourth article goes to matters concerning the states. The most important part of article four is the guarantee that each state will have a Republican form of government.

Article five establishes the amendment procedure. This was deliberately made difficult. The process of amending the Constitution should be understood by every citizen. Any power not specifically granted to the central government by the people still resides within the states or the people. By law this requires an amendment for the power to be taken and given to the federal government. Few of the modern usurpations of our federal government have the necessary constitutional backing.

Article number six defines the Constitution as the supreme law of the land. The federal government is given authority to make treaties which are binding in every state. All judges are bound to obey the Constitution as law. Article six also prescribes the official oath to support the Constitution to be taken by senators, representatives, state legislators and all executive and judicial officers, both federal and state. It is our responsibility to only elect those who have learned to be truthful and who consider an oath a sacred obligation. For them to not uphold the Constitution is a matter of fraud.

Article number seven explains the ratification process of the document itself.

Just seven simple and direct articles designed to limit government and thus protect the rights and sovereignty of every citizen and each state. This then is the genius of a document specifically designed to limit government to its proper function of protecting rights. It should have been enough if we had cared enough, or been wise enough, but the plundered wealth and politicians' promises have proven to be a great temptation to even freedom-loving Americans. The birthright is being sold for a mess of pottage.

There are only about twenty specific powers (Article 1, Section 8 U.S. Constitution) granted by the people to the federal government. All other responsibilities and rights usurped by centralized state control are illegal. Looking at fixed benchmarks we see how much is lost. The slowly rising red heat that may have initially felt a little warm and fuzzy cooks and kills our freedom. Metaphorically we are becoming another bowl of slow cooked frog soup.

A must-read book on this subject is, *America's 30 Years War,* by Balint Vazsonyi. Balint is a Hungarian-born historian, world renowned pianist, and observer of current events in the light of having personally lived through the control of Nazis and communists in his native land before adopting America as his home. Mr. Vazsonyi says this about the constitution:

> "That document is known as the Constitution of the United States. Nothing like it had ever existed. It was unique in the brevity and simplicity for a document of

such immeasurable significance; unique in the influence it acquired and has held in the hearts and minds of freedom-loving people around the world.

The framers of the Constitution understood the wisdom of making few laws. The fewer the laws, the broader the agreement. The broader the agreement, the less need for enforcement. The less enforcement, the less friction between government and the governed. And the less friction, the less waste of time and energy. The time and energy thus freed vastly increases people's creative capacity.

"That, in a nutshell, is the success story of the United States of America.

"The brevity of the Constitution may have an additional explanation. As noted, the Bible was the common denominator among all those who came together to frame the supreme secular law of the land. The founders understood that the faith, morality, and ethics embodied in God's law should form the basis of all man-made laws. And Americans everywhere understood that the Rule of Law should form the basis of the new nation."[10]

Good government is summarized as follows:

The independent and free person assumes the responsibilities of self-government under God. Rights associated with that responsibility are enjoyed. Love inspires this person to seek the same blessings for everyone. Expectations, faith, and confidence in the ability of others to also govern themselves are naturally extended. Because of this love for one's fellow men, we do not tolerate the injustice of ourselves or others being victimized. The force necessary, of self-defense and delegated self-defense are used to protect the individual's rights and sovereignty. This constitutes the sum of good government.

---

[10] Balint Vazsonyi, *America's Thirty Years War,* Regnery Publishing, Inc. Washington DC 1998 pg. 49-50.

The Economics of Love

When we look at the American miracle in terms of economic progression, it may be easy to overlook the key engine or force behind this drive. We approach the truth when we see freedom, liberty, independence, peace, responsibility, and justice. If, however, we do not see love as the pivotal core of success and greatness, we will fail to see the true America. The most sacred edifice where this love is nurtured and developed is the home. The attack against the American home and family is an attack against our economy. It is love that drives men to work harder, more creatively, and smarter, to increase their income, improve the comfort, convenience, and culture of their home. It is love that drives the wives and mothers to make the best of the available resources and devote countless hours in teaching, instructing, and building the character of children. All of the attributes of a great society are nurtured and practiced within the home. The power of love is the greatest power in the universe because it can harness, direct, and balance every other power or force in a creative and beneficial way. Without love, the power and force will be destructive. If we recognize this key truth we can recognize and reverse the destructive influences and cultivate and enhance the creative influences of our society. This is the key to improving our economy.

The love of power

Now that we have looked at love as the cornerstone of natural rights, responsibilities, and freedom, let's consider its opposite. It may be easy to confuse with words the difference between the love of power and the power of love, but the intent and especially the actions of their proponents are unmistakable. The love of power is inspired by an enmity, a despising for all that stands in the way of complete and immediate self-gratification. The greatest barrier to this gratification is the natural rights of others. This hatred is openly expressed, "We hate Christians and Christianity. Even the best of them must be considered our worst enemies. They preach love of one's

74

neighbor and mercy, which is contrary to our principles. Christian love is an obstacle to the development of the revolution. Down with love of our neighbor! What we want is hate...Only then can we conquer the universe."[11]

Only when we look at communism and socialism as a system of plunder and hatred do we finally see what it really is. Looking for a higher motivation or great truth in communism and socialism is like looking for lunch in the composting waste of a fine restaurant. You might find something to eat but it will only be a remnant of what you might find if you went in the front door.

For some strange reason, we tend to place a higher moralization on the actions of a group, or a government, than upon those of an individual. When we gain the wisdom of consistent thinking, we may rise above the power of lies told by those who love power. If it is wrong for me to take away your life, liberty, or property as an individual, why would I be justified in doing the same thing if I were part of a mob, or gang, or had been elected as a politician?

The ten planks of the Communist Manifesto
from an individual basis

Imagine your reaction if a neighbor came up to you and said that he would like you to participate in a new program to make the world better. The program has ten features that he is sure you will get excited about.

1. I will take all your land and charge you rent.
2. I will charge you a fee that I believe will keep you from ever having any excess with which to compete against my power.
3. I will become your only heir.
4. If you rebel, I will take all your belongings.
5. I will become your only bank and make all the rules for that bank.

---

[11] W. Cleon Skousen, *The Naked Communist*, Salt Lake City, Utah Reviewer 1958 pg. 350

6. I will control how you communicate with your other neighbors and your ability to travel.
7. I will be your boss and own all the means of production.
8. I will make you work.
9. I will move you wherever I want. If you give me trouble you might even find yourself trying to eke out a living on a frozen rock someplace.
10. I will become your child's teacher.

These proposals sound ludicrous, yet they are the essence of the ten planks of the Communist Manifesto. They are also the modern-day religion of state control, be it communism or socialism. The Marxist robber has not hidden the objectives of taking everything! If looked at closely we see the guiding influence behind the movement to destroy the Constitution through gradual usurpation.

Here they are, the ten planks of the Communist Manifesto by Marx:
1. Abolition of property in land and application of all rents of land to public purposes.
2. A heavy progressive or graduated income tax.
3. Abolition of all right of inheritance.
4. Confiscation of the property of all emigrants and rebels.
5. Centralization of credit in the hands of the state by means of a national bank with state capital and an exclusive monopoly.
6. Centralization of the means of communication and transport in the hands of the state.
7. Extension of factories and instruments of production owned by the state; the bringing into cultivation of waste lands, and the improvement of the soil generally in accordance with a common plan.
8. Equal obligation of all to work. Establishment of industrial armies, especially for agriculture.

9. Combination of agriculture with manufacturing industries; gradual abolition of the distinction between town and country by a more equable distribution of the population over the country.
10. Free education for all children in public schools. Abolition of child factory labor in its present form. Combination of education with industrial production, etc.

The fact that there are people who think like this is the very reason the rights of self-protection are so vital. We should get excited about this system, not to support it, but rather to protect ourselves against it. The better world sought by the Marxist robber is not for those they wish to control, but rather for themselves. It would be built upon the fruits of unjust confiscation. Is this not hatred? No one becomes a communist because they want to give all of these powers to someone else. Rather they want this power over someone else. Is this not injustice?

If all they really wanted was to surrender their own sovereignty, then a free society would serve them equally well. Would it be hard to individually find a dominator to whom to surrender one's rights and responsibilities? Two things we never see; a communist rally excited about the joys of being dominated by someone else, and a communist mob rushing about sharing what they have with the less fortunate.

Communism and socialism are defined by its ten basic planks proposed by Marx

All other Marxism is peripheral rhetoric to get the unwise to foolishly trade independence for their control. As we open our eyes and look at communism and socialism (two peas out of the same pod) we see not sublime greatness but rather the personal vendetta and hatred of the small, bitter, angry, and covetous. This jealousy and hatred drove the imagination to visualize the destruction and punishment of those whose goods were coveted.

77

Communism is not a great revolutionary movement of the downtrodden masses, but rather the self-centered indulgences of the immature whose meanness drives them to break and destroy all that does not personally and immediately gratify themselves.

The Communist Manifesto is a declaration of war against the rights of others

The proponents of these doctrines believe they are entitled to every right of individual sovereignty because of their own heightened and superior enlightenment. The rights of others are mere trivialities to be manipulated for a "greater good". The new man is not someone they want or intend to become but rather what they wish to "make someone else become". The rights they intend to deprive others of are the very rights they intend to continue using to bring themselves and keep themselves in power. The material utopia they envision is first to be taken and enjoyed by themselves and then, if there is any left after their lust and imagination has been completely satisfied, they will redistribute what is left back to the very people it was plundered from in the first place. There is power in the communistic movement, but it is the power of destruction. As a result, the power can only last as long as there is creation for it to cannibalize.

Communism and socialism alike in the end results

The Communist intends to take rights away at the point of a bayonet. The Socialist, on the other hand, has the delicate task of balancing his own lust with enough redistribution of plunder to deceive the morally immature to vote away the very same basic rights. They vote not only to give up their own rights, but also to use the police power of the state to forcibly take the rights of others. Communism and socialism are all about taking rights and making someone else responsible. The only difference between the two systems is how they intend to get to the same ultimate goal of total state control. The Communists believe in revolution and force to rob the rights. The Socialists believe in the slow and methodical moral corruption of the people to vote away the rights and give power to enforce that taking to the centralized state.

Marx's time period was full of injustice. What he proposed to replace it with was a greater injustice. There is a Biblical woe pronounced upon he who oppresses the hireling in his wages (Malachi 3:5). When the oppressions of any injustice become institutionalized, the peace of that society will be jeopardized. Injustice is what gives communism a foothold. Marx was a bitter, angry, and covetous man. His anger was focused upon a world that would not reward his pride and selfishness except he should demean himself by actual physical labor. His own self-worship required others to worship, or at least fear him, to be tolerated. Other people were merely pawns to be exploited. As a result, Marx never had any true friends.

Total irresponsibility demonstrated

There was one time in Marx's life that it appeared he might elevate himself through a tidy inheritance. Instead of paying his bills, elevating his family, or even redistributing it to his communistic comrades, the funds were immediately squandered on travel, drinking, and putting on the aristocratic airs he so hypocritically despised. He returned to his starving family only when the funds were completely gone. Thus we see the nefarious beginnings of a great evil system. As we look at the actual behavior of those elevated to power through communism, again and again we see the same abusive behavior. This adage is stated so well by British historian, Lord Action, "power tends to corrupt and absolute power corrupts absolutely". This is true of those seduced by the love of power.

We understand losing rights under the force of arms, but to vote one's freedoms away, even gradually, seems to be the epitome of irresponsibility and ignorance. If all actions of government and politician were given the acid test of how they stood in relation to the Constitution on one hand (the twenty responsibilities delegated to the federal government) and the ten planks of the Communist Manifesto on the other, the erosion of rights would be immediately and completely checked. After all, isn't this what the oath of office is all about? What a crime it is that most of what modern governments do is more slanted towards socialism or communism than the individual rights and responsibilities of a free people.

Socialism as a system of plunder

Let's now look at socialism (America's immediate threat) as a system of plunder as defined by the ten planks of the Communist Manifest. Any system of plunder can be identified. Look for any time the force of government is used to transfer a right, privilege, or wealth from the person who earned it to another who did not. The power of control is extracted by the centralized government as a brokerage fee for the transaction. The irony is that once the power to plunder has been centralized and the people desensitized to a system of injustice, it is only a matter of time until that same power and force will be used against every single individual within that society. Marx said, "The last capitalist we shall hang is the one that sold us the rope". It is never a question of if, only when. The plundering always begins with a minority that can be demonized and isolated before they are subjected to the plundering. This is accurately reflected by the statement by the Rev. Martin Niemoller under Hitler's socialistic Reich,

> "In Germany they came first for the Communists and I didn't speak up because I wasn't a Communist. Then they came for the Jews and I didn't speak up because I wasn't a Jew. Then they came for the trade unionists and I didn't speak up because I wasn't a trade unionist. Then they came for the Catholics and I didn't speak up because I was Protestant. Then they came for me–and by that time no one was left to speak up."[12]

---

[12] Niemdler Martin- A quote made frequently in public speeches during his lifetime. Simpson's Contemporary Quotations, Houghton Miffen Co. 1988 online www.bartleby.com/63/49/5249.html

Injustices and fear perpetrated by the communists and others were part of the reason the people accepted Hitler's false promise of security and peace. Fear of losing their own power and rights conditioned the people to allow the oppression of others. A government rarely, if ever, has the strength to plunder a neighboring country without first plundering people within its own boundaries.

The complete and utter plundering of Germany's Jews by Hitler was much more about plunder than race or ideology. The taking of their lives was the final act of stealing everything else. If the German people (and the world) had been moral enough to stop the plundering early, there never would have been a Second World War. The fruits of injustice are always a loss of peace.

The first three planks of the Communist Manifesto target society's most productive. It is particularly easy to demonize the wealthy if society has accepted institutionalized systems of injustice that give unfair advantages to the wealthy. If votes can be bought, justice sold, titles of nobility granted, or artificial barriers such as education and licensing used to restrict freedom and grant privilege unequally, then this injustice invites greater injustice.

Plundering usually starts with the wealthy. You get more return on your plundering effort by completely plundering a few rich than many poorer people. It is also easier to gather a mob of the less educated, less intelligent, and less responsible to help facilitate the plundering. In communism, the hateful mob physically accomplishes the plundering. In socialism, the mob votes and uses the police power of the state to facilitate the plundering. The first plank of the Manifesto, the abolition of property, is outright theft and confiscation. The second plank, a heavy progressive graduated income tax, is not only a form of theft but perpetuates the control of the state by assuring its monopoly on capital. The wise and unselfish Founders seem to have known that this would be the evil tool with which the lovers of power were most likely to begin their plundering.

Our current tax system-not part of the plan

Not only does Article 1 Section 9 of the Constitution specifically forbid any direct tax except in proportion to the census, but in Article number 5 (the amending process), Congress was specifically forbidden to amend this section anytime prior to 1888. The 16th Amendment created Constitutional disunity. The Constitution first forbids this type of tax, and then has an amendment allowing it. This type of tax creates the illusion everyone actually works for the government. A constant vigilance is required by every citizen to do the required bookkeeping. A host of governmental overseers are employed to assure compliance. The privacy, sanctity, and sovereignty of the individual are subordinated. The tax itself becomes the enforcement tool for behavior modification and control. If a person after his departure from this life found himself still required to file a 1040 there would be little doubt which way he had gone. Nothing says "pursuit of happiness" in quite the same way as dealing with the IRS.

The limited government envisioned by the nation's founders could easily maintain itself with the tariffs collected by a few collectors and at entry ports. If a society still wanted to maintain a high level of governmental service, a national sales tax collected by the states would free the taxpayer from the oppressive burden of government intrusion, greatly reduce the collection costs, restore a degree of state's rights, and eliminate the need for the 16th Amendment.

An attack on American production

One of the biggest reasons to eliminate the IRS and personal income tax is that it really is an attack on American production. Originally, only foreign goods were taxed for the privilege of being sold in the American marketplace. The income tax, as a tax on production of American goods, raises the price of every article produced by American labor. These goods then have to compete with goods produced in other countries which pay no American tax for the labor used to produce them. This un-level playing field is one reason there has been such a loss of American jobs. Lovers of power fight to keep the graduated income tax at all costs because the power to tax is the power to control! Control is what power is all about.

Regulation, a barrier to innovation

Probably the most expensive aspect of regulation is that it is a barrier to innovation. Innovation is the key reason that the order of Heaven is accompanied by the blessings of Heaven. There is an innovative answer to every problem that has, or will ever plague mankind. Free people think. Free people act. This is the formula for innovation. Controllers who love power have little tolerance for free thought in others. Free thought leads people to see beyond the big lies. This is why whenever communists or socialists acquire power; they purge society of free thinkers through murder, plunder, or terror.

The greatest danger of a control-based society that stifles innovation and creativity is the danger to the society itself. Often, a huge problem or difficulty may be just an inconvenience to a free society. The collective thinking, creativity, and problem solving ability of all free people produces many answers, implements those answers, and evaluates and gives priority to the most effective solutions. An example is how free people overcame the Y-2-K problem. This is far different from the limited innovation of a controlled society which may succumb to a much lesser problem. This is why so much of what occurs in these societies appears so primitive and backwards to free people. This is also why these controlled societies are so reliant upon espionage, industrial theft, and transferred wealth to prop up their diminishing economies. It is hard to fathom why there is such a drive to force us to follow the destructive lead of these faltering kingdoms, until we see that there are those who would rather rule over ruin than participate in prosperity.

Regulation, as a percentage of gross, costs small start-up businesses hundreds of times what it costs big businesses. All knowledge necessary to comply with regulation must be acquired, usually by one person. This wastes the energy and creativity of the start-up entrepreneur. The oppressive fear of the costs of an honest, but ignorant, mistake stifles many of the blessings of innovation we could be enjoying. Even after the initial start up, cost of regulation (as a percentage of gross) costs small business an estimated five times what it costs big business. In spite of the rhetoric, regulation is the friend of big business.

Inheritance Tax–Biblically Wrong

The third plank of the Manifesto abolishes rights of inheritance (usually accomplished through an inheritance tax). Not only is this a means of plunder, but it destroys the continuity of families. If government is to be perceived as the all-providing god of the people, then an appreciation for the creating, building, and transferred love, which comes through inheritance, cannot be tolerated. As seen by the hypocritical Marx, this is only to be applied by force to other people, not practiced by himself. There is a Biblical woe (a curse from God) pronounced upon those who practice this oppression against the widow and the fatherless (Zechariah 7:10).

National Bank, not Constitutional, but is Marxist

The fifth plank of the Manifesto, a National Bank to centralize credit and issue currency, represents one of the greatest opportunities for the usurpation of power ever conceived. The control of a nation's currency comes close to financial control of the nation. There is a sacred marriage covenant between a people and its government. Government has the responsibilities of protecting the rights of the people. The people have the responsibilities of supporting their leaders. This is a wonderful relationship when covenants are kept and love and service are controlling influences. There is a Biblical description of an opposing system. John the Revelator describes the great last day's usurper and controller he calls the great whore. What begins with an act of fornication with government ends up with the whore ruling over the kings of the Earth (Revelation Chapter 17). Imagine the confusion to a social order, the indignity suffered, and injustice, in a threesome marriage relationship consisting of a husband, wife, and a whore. Every secret or open act between a marriage partner and a whore affects the rights of the other marriage partner. This imagery is powerful and relevant.

Taxation without representation

Constitutionally, the union of government and a national bank is an illegal act. The Revolutionary War was fought over the issue of taxation without representation. As long as the government is reliant upon the people for its support and the people are secure in their rights then each has great incentive to work for the benefit of the other. When the government no longer grants representation to the people being taxed then government can pursue its own selfish interests irrespective of the rights of the people. People feel they are no longer represented even though they do not always know exactly why or how. Whenever the money supply is increased the people pay the tax of inflation. There is no representation over this tax. Looked at another way, a nation's currency is somewhat akin to stock certificates for the business conducted within that country. In any publicly traded stock issuing company, any person who could control when, and how much stock was issued, could also control the value of stock and ultimately control that company. The lovers of power know this simple truth, but go to great lengths to conceal their covert usurpation. Thomas Jefferson's writings on this subject are particularly clear and relevant on this subject.

Marxist Slavery

The sixth, seventh, eighth, and ninth planks of the manifesto also define the boundaries of slavery. Control of communication and travel, state ownership of all means of production, obligation to work and control of where people live make the individual little more than chattel to be exploited. Personal growth and improvement, happiness and joy, accomplishment and the learning experience of failure are traded for the false security of state control.

Indoctrination of children

The tenth plank of the Marxist Manifesto is the most hateful and destructive of all because of what it does to the future. The communist will abolish all rights and take everything by force and fear, so taking children can be subordinated to the tenth plank. The Socialist, on the other hand, who works to arrive at the same ultimate goal of state control and believes in the same ten planks, sees that the tenth plank is the most important. The great evil intent is hidden by what can be perceived as a worthy goal: free education for all children in state schools.

What is the cost of free education that dethrones the loving God of Heaven and exalts man without eternal truth, religion, and morality, as the only true God? What is the cost of free education that replaces God and the order and majesty of the universe with the doctrine of chance? What is the cost of free education that debases man to the level of mere animal instincts, urges, and materialistic selfishness? What is the cost of free education that teaches rights before responsibility and justice, dependency above independence, and peace and control, above freedom and liberty? What is the cost of free education that isn't really free after all?

If responsibility to teach a nation's children is transferred from the parents to the state, then every other responsibility and right are in danger of following. The wicked genius of National Socialism (NAZI) in Germany knew this. Hitler stated:

"When an opponent declares, 'I will not come over to your side, I calmly say, 'Your child belongs to us already...What are you? You will pass on. Your descendants, however, now stand in the new camp. In a short time they will know nothing else but this new community." And on May 1, 1937, he declared, "This new Reich will give its youth to no one, but will itself take youth and give to youth its own education and its own upbringing."[13]

The lovers of power who have aligned themselves with the socialistic or communistic movement or its principles know that power over the children will eventually translate to power over the adults of a society. A generation is not too long to wait.

Great Teachers slow the tide

In America, the trend has been greatly slowed by a number of great members of our society who are motivated by the power of love and have chosen teaching (one of the most honorable professions) as a career. These valiant teachers are handicapped in many ways from teaching what is most valuable and dear to them, but what they are speaks so loudly that many youth get the message.

These great teachers could do so much more for our youth under a system with freedom and liberty to teach what is of most worth, but what they do under the oppression of money and state control is commendable. Imagine teaching our history from the words of the great men and women who lived it, who sacrificed to build a better world, and who invariably saw the hand of God in the events unfolding before them. Imagine teaching science in light of the great order of the universe instead of having to bend reality to see chance in everything. Imagine teaching social science in light of freedom and liberty, independence and peace, responsibility and justice that has made America great, instead of the socialistic and humanistic concepts that have failed to produce greatness anywhere.

Education should be seen as an opportunity

Imagine teaching children who realize education is a

---

[13] William L. Shirer, *The Rise and Fall of the Third Reich*, Simon and Schuster, New York 1960 pg. 249

privilege. Children who know their parents love them enough to take responsibility and the attending rights to see their children taught the very way they themselves would want to be taught. Children are smart enough to know that a privilege is something that is optional and valuable. If you have to use force (the law) to make someone accept something, then it must not really be that valuable. This is like politicians telling adults about the "privilege" of paying exorbitant taxes so responsibilities and rights can be taken away from them. This is also the reason for the high burn-out among public school teachers. More pay is hardly just compensation for the thankless job of being the front line of state control. Private school teachers, employed by responsible parents, typically earn less but report higher job satisfaction. They accomplish more statistically with their children than do their public school counterparts. There is also a tremendous financial burden for some parents to pay double when they are taxed to support public education and paying additionally to educate their own. The immediate and eternal rewards to themselves and children however may be incalculable.

The only way to regain the rights and blessing of educating our children is to demand the return of the responsibilities. It is not just to seek a right without the responsibility. There are great blessings, rights, and parental privileges that cannot be transferred to others. Neither should the responsibilities be transferred. Nowhere else is the power of love so greatly manifested as in the art of teaching. We can hardly afford the loss and costs associated with allowing teaching to be controlled by those who are motivated by the love of power.

THE BILL OF RIGHTS- MOTIVATED BY LOVE

Are we wise enough to realize our love for our fellow men must translate into a respect for their individual sovereignty? We are justified in expecting and requiring the protection of our own individual rights and sovereignty only if we treat others the same way. No greater manifestation of love for God, ourselves, and others, exists than this. Once this pretext is lost, then any excuse for the "need" for more government will do.

The real differences between governments are not the ideological differences between the various "isms" but difference between guaranteed individual sovereignty, protected by the law of limited governments, or the loss of individual sovereignty under unlimited government. True, there may be tremendous differences in the amount of oppression or freedom allowed by a tyrant or a just king. The point is that it all boils down to generosity or restriction based on whims, and not law. Each loss of responsibility and rights becomes a spring board for the next usurpation. This process can occur rapidly, as in Nazi Germany or a communistic take-over, or may take considerably longer as is occurring in America's socialist welfare state.

Only love, coupled with understanding, has power to reverse this process. Each of the rights guaranteed within the Bill of Rights is a gift from God. God trusts His children with great power and great responsibility. The weak and shallow assume the answer to the misuse of power is to keep power from the people. The great and gracious know power and responsibility are necessary parts of growth and progression. The answer is to teach, love, and lift others, while strictly requiring accountability for every power, right, or responsibility. From a young age and upward everyone should learn if you abuse a power or right, you lose that power or right. This should form the underlying strategy of our entire court system. Tying rights with the direct responsibility makes sense. For instance, a shoplifter could lose the privilege of going into stores without identifying himself to the owner and asking permission to enter. This learning process is more efficient and beneficial to the individual and society than limiting the power and punishing the potential.

As long as people prefer the promises of state control to the truth of freedom, they will continue to forge the chains of their own slavery. The early chains of slavery are ignorance and selfishness. These are followed by dependency and control, which lead to fear and oppression. To expect a society raised in ignorance and selfishness to remain free, is to expect that which never has been and never can be.

The Bill of Rights is a restriction on government, not a granting of rights by government

The original draft of the Constitution did not contain the Bill of Rights. The Founders were well schooled in the principles of natural law and did not want to make any pretext that somehow they or any government had the power to grant rights. They knew that if it was ever accepted that the government had the power to grant rights then certainly the same government would also have the power to limit rights. The Constitution merely transferred from the people about twenty very limited powers to the government. No authority was given to infringe upon any of the rights enumerated within the Bill of Rights. It was felt that if rights were granted within the Constitution, the government could begin, by interpretation, to limit those rights. Also, any rights or powers not granted to the individual by the government could then be assumed the domain of the federal government. Their fears have proven to be justified. On the other hand, one Constitutional delegate, Col. Mason of Virginia, stated that he would rather cut off a hand than accept a Constitution without a Bill of Rights.

In many ways, the Bill of Rights has proven to be invaluable as the last bastion of defense for individual sovereignty. A satisfactory solution was found in the wording, "Congress shall make no law..." thus making the Bill of Rights a restriction upon government, rather than a granting of rights by the government. Under natural law and the principles of justice, it is wrong for any individual to take any of the rights enumerated in the bill of rights from any other person. If the individual is not justified in this taking, how can he possibly delegate that power to the government? The answer is that it cannot be given; only stolen.

The lovers of power will go to great lengths to exploit or create the circumstances to justify the assumptions of power they covet. For this reason eternal vigilance is part of the price of liberty. The Bill of Rights is a declaration of individual sovereignty and independence. It is the antitheses of the Marxist planks of the manifesto. Every Marxist or dictatorial usurpation must correspondingly infringe upon one or more of the articles of the Bill of Rights, or with the basic rights of life, liberty, and property that the Constitution was meant to protect.

Love central to establishing Individual Sovereignty and The Kingdom of God on Earth

From the model of the Heavenly ideals of order and agency we used earlier, we see that the power of love is the central feature in the establishment of the order of Heaven on Earth. The laws of justice are balanced by love with the responsibility of the individual. The independence of the individual is balanced by love with the peace of society. The freedom of the individual is balanced by love with the liberty of society. The love of others is balanced by the love of self. This is manifested in individual sovereignty and the protection of individual sovereignty in others.

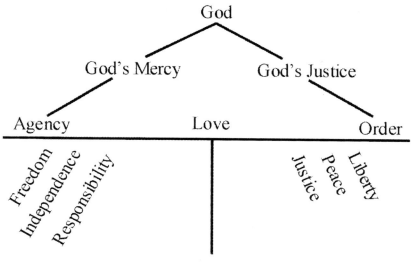

God

God's Mercy   God's Justice

Agency   Love   Order

Freedom Independence Responsibility   Justice Peace Liberty

Individual Sovereignty

CONCEPT SUMMARY

Individual sovereignty is protected using rights of self-protection and delegated powers (government) of self protection. Correct government must have a foundation of justice and protect from injustice. It takes unity and organization to check those whose love of power motivates them to take rights, responsibilities, and individual sovereignty of others. The power of love is what secures and reestablishes individual sovereignty.

The fourth principle of just representation is the unleashing and promotion of the power of love and the recognition and protection from its opposite, the love of power.

CONCEPT NUMBER FIVE
THE LAW

"And it is easier for heaven and earth to pass than one tittle of the law to fall."

-Luke 16:17

Our Republic was built upon the foundation of the eternal principles of the great laws. The restoration of our Republic will come as slowly or as quickly as we return to that foundation. The laws of God are eternal with Him. When we honor God's laws, we honor Him. When we ignore God's laws, we lose the blessings of liberty, peace, and justice.

There has probably never been a greater or more concise treatment of the principles of eternal law vs. the very same socialist-communist ideas and plans that plague us today than the short book, *The Law*, written by Frederic Bastiat in June of 1850. Bastiat's prophetic words not only warned the French people of the impending downfall of their once great nation if they continued the course and adopted the complete socialism sweeping their nation, but he also warned the people of America of the two central issues of the upcoming civil war.

Bastiat's, *The Law*
"There is no country in the world where the law is kept more within its proper domain: the protection of every person's liberty and property. As a consequence of this, there appears to be no country in the world where the social order rests on a firmer foundation. But even in the United States, there are two issues--and only two–that have always endangered the public peace.

"What are these two issues? They are slavery and tariffs. These are the only two issues where, contrary to the general spirit of the Republic of the United States, law has assumed the character of a plunderer.

"Slavery is a violation, by law, of liberty. The protective

94

tariff is a violation, by law, of property.

"It is a most remarkable fact that this double legal crime–a sorrowful inheritance from the Old World–should be the only issue which can, and perhaps will, lead to the ruin of the Union. It is indeed impossible to imagine, at the very heart of a society, a more astounding fact than this: The law has come to be an instrument of injustice.   And if this fact brings terrible consequences to the United States–where the proper purpose of the law has been perverted only in the instances of slavery and tariffs–what must be the consequences in Europe, where the perversion of the law is a principle; a system?"[14]

Note that Bastiat's observation of only two violations of the principles of natural law was made in 1850. Today the list of violations is a lengthy one.

Every freedom and liberty loving individual should frequently treat themselves to this great work. The beginning and ending of Bastiat's book seem particularly inspired:

> "The law perverted! And the police powers of the state perverted along with it! The law, I say, not only turned from its proper purpose but made to follow an entirely contrary purpose! The law become the weapon of every kind of greed! Instead of checking crime, the law itself guilty of the evils it is supposed to punish!"[15]

At the ending of the book is this analogy for those who would tamper with the law:

> "...a celebrated traveler arrived one day in the midst of a tribe of savages, where a child had just been born. A crowd of soothsayers, magicians, and quacks–

---

[14] Frederic Bastiat, *The Law*, Dean Russell Translation Irvington-on-Hudson, New York 21st printing 1996 pg. 18-19 The Foundation for Economic education Inc.

[15] Ibid p. 1

armed with rings, hooks, and cords–surrounded it. One said: 'This child will never see the sunshine unless I slant his eyes.' Another said: 'He will never stand upright unless I bend his legs.' A fifth said: 'He will never learn to think unless I flatten his skull.'

"Stop,' cried the traveler. 'What God does is well done. Do not claim to know more that He. God has given organs to this frail creature; let them develop and grow strong by exercise, use, experience, and liberty.'

"God has given to men all that is necessary for them to accomplish their destinies. He has provided a social form as well as a human form. And these social organs of persons are so constituted that they will develop themselves harmoniously in the clean air of liberty. Away, then, with quacks and organizers! Away with their artificial systems! Away with the whims of governmental administrators, their socialized projects, their centralization, their tariffs, their government schools, their state religions, their free credit, their bank monopolies, their regulations, their restrictions, their equalization by taxation, and their pious moralizations!

"And now that the legislators and do-gooders have so futilely inflicted so many systems upon society, may they finally end where they should have begun: May they reject all systems, and try liberty; for liberty is an acknowledgment of faith in God and His works."[16]

Pride before the fall

So what is our basic character flaw that allows us to so flippantly ignore the underlying principles of God's Law? The answer is pride. We are not talking about the modern misuse of the word where pride may mean anything from being pleased with something's goodness, to joy of association, patriotism, or even love. We refer, rather to the Biblical use of the term where

---

[16] Ibid pp. 74-75

it is always something profoundly evil. This Biblical pride is something based entirely on selfishness. It is an arrogance fueled by enmity that puts self-interest above all else, including God. This self-exalting pride always leads to a type of blindness that makes a fall inevitable. There is probably no greater manifestation of pride than a person who thinks of himself as a lawmaker.

The laws of sound government, justice, freedom, mercy, love, light, truth, and association are all eternal with the Being we look up to and call "Father". A scientist would never be so arrogant as to think of himself as capable of making the laws of nature. Science has been so wonderfully successful because of its system for discovering, proving, and utilizing the eternal laws of nature for the benefit of mankind. Imagine the chaos if science was inundated with 'lawmakers'. Imagine if the humility, respect, and honor science has cultivated for the laws of nature were to suddenly be replaced with the type of pride so prevalent today in our nation's capital. Imagine a system that instead of utilizing the accumulated and proven wisdom of the ages, accepted truth as a relative thing, constantly changing and based not upon a great underlying order but rather upon the whims of the scientist doing the experiments. Imagine the amount of time to be wasted arguing, with no common ground of understanding, that such a system would impose.

Statesmen are Judges

The alternative to the concept of the modern lawmakers is the ancient Biblical concept of the judge. When Israel received the blessings and responsibilities of self-rule, their leaders were known as judges. The respect and authority resided in the seat of authority and not the person. It was humbly understood that they were acting on behalf of him (God) to whom the seat belonged. Their position was not to make the laws, but to judge and apply the laws for the benefit of those whom they were called to serve. A promise was given that those who studied and kept God's law would be known as the wise.

"Keep therefore and do them; for there is your wisdom and your understanding in the sight of the nations, which shall hear all these statutes, and say, Surely this great nation is a wise and understanding people" (Deuteronomy 4:6).

A miracle occurs when we put aside our own will to stand in proxy for the Higher Judge. We may do this imperfectly at first, but this is a part of growing up. Children emulate and follow their parents to grow up physically. We emulate and follow the Redeemer to grow up spiritually. The promise is that when Christ comes we shall be like Him for we shall see Him as He is (1 John 3:2).

This is a major part of the miracle of the Kingdom of God extending to the Earth. All miracles have both an Earthly and physical part as well as a spiritual and Heavenly part. The Earthly part of this miracle is what we do. The spiritual part is that, with the recognition that the calling is not about us, coupled with a humble submission and seeking the Father's will, there comes a divine mantel of approval, and helpful, inspired guidance. Thus, His will is done on Earth as it is in Heaven and we have God's justice upon the Earth. Christ taught that this is how even He labored.

> "I can of mine own self do nothing: as I hear, I judge: and my judgment is just: because I seek not mine own will but the will of the Father which hath sent me" (John 5:30).

What a blessing it will be when all who represent us are just men who recognize the eternal nature of the laws of justice. Man must learn that his place is under the law, not over it. Then we will seek the wisdom to judge from our great lawgiver (not law makers) and try to understand the laws in light of scripture, history, science, the study of God's creations, and through direct inspiration and revelation. Our judges truly will be wise men.

Pride destroys Freedom

Discovering and utilizing eternal law is not always an easy task, but it will be infinitely easier than trying to govern by trying to make laws. This will bring a great journey full circle. This journey began long ago when the God of Heaven sent His spiritual offspring on a great adventure. He first made His children free and then gave us laws to keep us free. The wise use of freedom and acceptance of these laws is the journey that brings us back again to God and our home.

The other area where pride has had a terribly damaging influence upon our Republic is going to hit much closer to home for most of us. A prayer is offered that the reader, as a child of God, will prepare his or her heart to receive a loving rebuke and a call for help to undo this damage.

Thomas Jefferson, who was one of the greatest statesmen to have ever lived, penned the powerful words of the Declaration of Independence. The beauty of eternal truths contained in this document ring true and is spiritually carried to the very heart and core of freedom-loving people everywhere. These words inspired a whole nation to rise up against tyranny, pledge their lives, their fortunes, and their sacred honor for the cause, and throw off the yoke of bondage. They did it for themselves and as a birthright and heritage for generations yet unborn. From this document we read these great words:

> "We hold these truths to be self-evident, that all men are created equal, that they are endowed by their Creator with certain unalienable rights, that among these are life, liberty, and the pursuit of happiness. That, to secure these rights, governments are instituted among men, deriving their just powers from the consent of the governed..."

The last line contains a powerful truth that must be understood in the context of the whole paragraph. Many have misunderstood this line to mean that in America the majority rules. This is far from the spirit and intent in this document. The intent of the Founding Fathers was to build a Republic based upon the principles of God's laws and the acceptance of God as the ultimate High King of the land.

Democracy established in Pride

If majority rules, where does that leave God? Pride that allows a politician to think himself a lawmaker is the same pride that allows a group of people to think they have a complete right to become the law. They seek to use the force of government to take what they want if they can get enough of a mob to become the majority. Pure democracy has been defined as two wolves and a sheep getting together to decide what is for lunch. Madison, who is considered the father of the Constitution, has this to say about democracy:

> "Democracies have ever been spectacles of turbulence and contention; have ever been found incompatible with personal security or the rights of property; and have in general been as short in their lives as they have been violent in their deaths."[17]

Pure democracy is centered on the humanistic view of man as the center of the universe, thus whatever man does is right. Self-worship is at the heart of destruction which our constitutional Republic has suffered. In order to enthrone democracy, we must first dethrone God. The logic goes like this; if there is no God, then we are not responsible to Him and there is no right or wrong, only choices. In this scenario, the fairest way to accomplish anything is majority rule. If a man is important, then surely whatever the majority decides is most important. Herein lays the seeds of discord and disharmony. Under pure democracy equality is impossible. If all rights stem from being part of the majority and ultimately everyone is a minority of one,

---

[17] James Madison "National Gazette" January 19th, 1792.

then that minority of one is always pitted against the majority of many.

Seen from another direction, all evil is rooted in selfishness. Selfishness is characterized by an, "I will take" attitude. An individual is faced with many difficulties that require deception, concealment, and great effort to un-rightfully take. This is the great appeal of the "gang". Usually the biggest gang can affect the biggest take. This explains much of the degeneration of American politics. Taking what is not right to take is always considered a grave offence in the sight of God, regardless of whether the taking has been voted on or not. It has rightfully been observed that democracies can only last until the majority of voters discover that they can vote themselves plunder from the public treasury. Injustice will destroy peace, and that will curtail liberty. This offends God who so lovingly and patiently offers the order of Heaven to man. Injustice is at the very core of pure democracy.

We are not a democracy

At the end of the Constitutional Convention, a question was asked. "Mr. Franklin, what [kind of government] have you wrought us?" He replied, "A Republic, if you can keep it." To illustrate how the concept has been lost, in a speech given on the birthday of our Constitution for the year 2000, President Bill Clinton misquoted the phrase by saying, "A Democracy, if you can keep it." We must know the difference if we are to appreciate the difference. If we do not stand for our Republic, our Republic will not stand. Pure Democracy is the natural enemy of a Constitutional Republic.

A Republic is government based upon law. Pure Democracy is simply majority rule. The American system, as proposed by its founders, is a Republic based upon the natural and eternal principles of justice, equality, and individual sovereignty, established and judged by just representatives chosen by the people. Each leg of this tri-foundation is of vital importance to the protection of freedom and liberty. In order of importance, these legs are:

First—the Republic, based upon God's law.
Second—the judgment of just representatives.
Third—the righteous voice of the people.

If any single leg of this tri-foundation becomes corrupted, the other two may still be able to maintain justice. If all three become corrupted, then justice is destroyed, peace is lost, and liberty is not possible.

A heavy moral cloud overshadows the concept of pure democracy. The true political scientist can see the seeds of self-destruction and inefficiency of a purely democratic institution. Our Constitutional Republic utilizes democratic vote, but in order of importance, this is only third. Consider this hypothetical situation.

A modern parable

A kind and wise businessman, who had built a large, efficient, and wonderfully successful organization, decided to retire. Since he had acquired all he would ever need, he decided to generously give the business to his beloved employees. The business was readily equipped with every resource that should be necessary for its continued success. Instructions were left that the business was to be run for the benefit of all employees, and that wise, hardworking, honest people of integrity are to be chosen to run the business according to the tried and proven method shown to be so successful. The employees were to gather in small groups and choose the best people to represent them. These representatives would then choose a committee to study and call a person to run the company with the committee retaining the accountability and responsibility of reporting back to the employees. Under this system we would expect the business to continue on successfully with each employee feeling represented and a part of the system.

Now imagine the same scenario except that one of the

employees decides that he would like the benefits of being president and that this might be his only chance to gain the position's benefits and glory for himself. He begins this effort like a despot preparing to go for the spoils of war. He even manages the effort like a war campaign. Indeed, a battle is what is planned. The language and speech of war is used and lavish plans are laid to reward his supporters and punish his opposition. His first matter of business is to convince the employees that the previous owner is out of the picture, and it is rightfully their company. They (the majority) should choose a president any way they want. With this accomplished, others decide that they too would like to be president, some for honorable reasons, some for not as honorable reasons. With this, the battle begins to heat up.

One can now imagine the scenario to follow. Every kind of outlandish promise is made. Workers are promised shorter working hours, less work, more pay, less supervision, college for their children, free lunch, and all the benefits of management without the responsibility. Management is promised more money, power, prestige, office furnishing, etc. In order to pay for the excessive costs of running the campaign, money is sought outside the organization. Suppliers are promised better terms and higher prices in exchange for financial contributions. Even competitors are approached with promises not to compete in some ways, for support of the campaign. Future profits are mortgaged, retirement funds compromised, and the work place changed from one of peace and harmony to one of constant negativism. The candidates make a spectacle of their effort to discredit each other and promote their own shallow agenda.

Which business would be expected to prosper or even survive? Which would benefit the employees, customers, or the world the most? The answer is ludicrously obvious.

103

Marx believed that raising democracy to the level of political supremacy is the first step of a communist take over

"We have seen above that the first step in a revolution by the working class is to raise the proletariat to the position of ruling class, to establish democracy.

"The proletariat will use its political supremacy to wrest by degrees all capital from the bourgeoisie, to centralize all instruments of production in the hands of the state..."

-Communist Manifesto

The Founding Fathers foresaw all of these problems inherent in a democratic system. To illustrate the problem, consider asking most Americans this simple question. In America, the majority rules, true or false? Most will quickly answer true. If asked to elaborate they will usually say because we are a democracy. We have been conditioned to accept the doctrine of Karl Marx and the first step towards destroying the Republic. The correct answer should be; in America the law rules. We try to make our law as close to God's law as possible, meaning, ultimately, God rules. We are a Republic. We use democratic principles to elect leaders to judge according to the law.

Three important checks against tyranny that have been seriously eroded are:

1. A Republic based on law. Jefferson stated "Confidence is everywhere the parent of despotism... In questions of power, then let no more be said of confidence in man, but bind him down from mischief by the chains of the constitution."[18] The law of our Republic has been circumvented by simply choosing

---

[18] Thomas Jefferson, *Kentucky Resolutions* 1798 Quoted from The Real Thomas Jefferson Part II prepared by Richard Maxfield, K. DeLynn Cook, and W. Cleon Skousen, National Center for Constitutional studies, Washington DC 1981 pg. 382

to ignore the Constitution, or by interpreting it out of existence.

2. A system of checks and balances. Our constitutional form of government incorporates many checks and balances. Many are being circumvented or lost. The original Constitution called for the US Senate to be elected by the state legislatures, the purpose being that this body would represent the rights of the states and be a moderating influence upon what they expected to be a more radical and democratic House of Representatives. This has been circumvented by the 17th amendment ratified April 8th, 1915. The negative effect has been a more democratic America. The problems seen in the second business scenario are America's problems today. The result is the loss of state's rights, the loss of individual freedoms and liberties, and the centralization of control.

3. A system of just representation. Jefferson did not use the name just representation proposed by this author, but the concepts are his. Jefferson's system was not fully implemented. The last remaining vestige of this system is the Electoral College. This has been circumvented by making the Electoral College impotent. The cry of the politician today is to completely abolish the Electoral College.

Harmony of concepts

Now let us return to the paragraph in the Declaration of Independence which seems to justify democracy. The truths are "self-evident". The concepts in the first paragraph are not to be sacrificed and voided so that pure democracy can be implemented. Just because governments derive their just powers from the consent of the governed, does not mean that democracy is the only way to accomplish this consent. The beauty of the original Constitution, coupled with Jefferson's concepts to be

105

discussed in more detail later in this book, is that both concepts can be complementary instead of antagonistic to each other.

If we look closely, we see not a description of unlimited government by majority rule, but actually very limited government upon the basis of natural law. What is natural law? Natural law is based upon natural order, stated in the Declaration of Independence. This order is;

#1. Men are created.
#2. They are equal because of the equality of rights endowed by their Creator.
#3. These rights include life, liberty, and the ability to use these (coupled with our energy, ingenuity, intelligence, and property) to pursue happiness.
#4. Governments are created to secure these rights.
#5. Just government's authority is limited to that authority delegated to government by the consent of the governed.

Rights, Property, and the Law

Governments exist because people have rights. People are created equal in respect to law by God. If government infringes upon any one of the three enumerated rights (life, liberty, or property acquired in the pursuit of happiness) at that moment it becomes unjust and an offense to the God who created man and his equality under law. The three rights are each dependant upon each other and each is impossible without the other two. The term "pursuit of happiness" means individual self-determination. We are not to be oppressed by government, unjust law, or a collective view of what that happiness is to be.

Rights come from God to man. Governments are created because man delegates some rights to the government. It is not then legal under the laws of justice for government to possess power over any individual that exceeds the delegated rights.

Property and wealth defined is the ability to take natural resources (provided by God) and turn them through expended effort into things useful or necessary for man. How we use

106

property and wealth is the pursuit of happiness. Property is produced as an extension of a man's life and liberty. Property rights are absolutely essential to the preservation of life and liberty. Life, liberty, and property cannot be separated. They are inalienable as man's rights to preserve. Frederic Bastiat puts it this way:

"What then is law? It is the collective organization of the individual right to lawful defense.

"Each of us has a natural right–from God–to defend his person, his liberty, and his property. These are the three basic requirements of life, and the preservation of any one of them is completely dependent upon the preservation of the other two. For what are our faculties but the extension of our individuality? And what is property but an extension of our faculties?

"If every person has the right to defend–even by force– his person, his liberty, and his property, then it follows that a group of men have the right to organize and support a common force to protect these rights constantly."[19]

Rights come from God

Rights are secure only upon acknowledgment of their being recognized as gifts from God. Our Founding Fathers understood this.

Thomas Jefferson asked:

"Can the liberties of a nation be thought secure when we have removed their only firm basis, a conviction in the minds of the people that these liberties are of the gift of God? That they are not to be violated but with his wrath?"[20]

---

[19] Frederic Bastiat, *The Law*, pg. 6
[20] Ezra Taft Benson, *The Constitution, A Heavenly Banner*. Deseret Book Co. Salt Lake City Utah 1986 pg. 5

Thomas Paine wrote:

"Rights are not gifts from one man to another, nor from one class of men to another. ...It is impossible to discover any origin of rights otherwise than in the origin of man; it consequently follows that rights appertain to man in right of his existence, and must therefore be equal to every man."[21]

Humility holds the law in place

Once we see that pride and covetousness are the driving force behind inequality, we can open our eyes to see that true humility is the basis of all equality under the law. Some mistakenly label greatness and confidence as pride and any submission and weakness as humility. Neither is accurate. There is a confidence that only comes through true humility. Humility is gratitude stemming from understanding. This humility leads to the faith that brings success and greatness. Humility is the strength that establishes and holds the law in place. Humility is the conduit through which the power and strength of God are manifest. English author, John Ruskin, put it this way:

"The first test of a truly great man is humility. I do not mean by humility doubt of his own power...[but really] great men...have a curious...feeling that greatness is not in them, but through them...and they see something divine...in every other man...and are endlessly, foolishly and incredibly merciful."[22]

OUR OPPORTUNITY AND RESPONSIBILITY TO THE WORLD IN THE LAST DAYS

One of Isaiah's most remarkable and profound prophecies

---

[21] Ibid pg 5

[22] *Works of John Ruskin*, edited by ET Cook and Alexander Wedderbury 29th Volume 1903-12, 5:331. Quoted from a speech by Marlin K. Jenson March 31st, 2001, Salt Lake City, Utah

of the last days is found in Isaiah 2:2-4. A special place is designated, referred to as the mountain of the Lord's house (not just a city on a hill, but a whole mountain). This mountain will draw people from all nations like a magnet. People will want to come here to learn God's ways and walk in His paths. From this place will go forth God's law. We see from history that this is a prophecy of America. The United States Constitution is the world's first written constitution. This document has become the pattern. Nearly every nation has a written constitution and their pattern usually is this great American document. Unfortunately, America's pattern of ignoring the foundation of God's law contained in the Constitution is also followed. The prophecy reveals in the last days the word of the Lord will go forth from Jerusalem. We see in a remarkable fashion that the Bible has flooded the Earth. Every nation involved in the great work of extending the Bible's reach to the entire world has been greatly blessed. The better a nation is at carrying the Bible, the more it is blessed. Think about it. When Spain was the world leading exporter of Biblical Christianity, they were the world's leading super power. Columbus stated in a letter to a friend:

> "I feel persuaded, by the many and wonderful manifestations of Divine Providence in my especial favor, that I am the chosen instrument of God in bringing to pass a great event-no less than the conversion of millions who are now existing in the darkness of Paganism."[23]

Success tied to Christianity

When limited Christianity from Spain meant less to the people than the exported oppression and violation of the principles of God's law, Spain lost it all. Many historians have judged Columbus harshly for this oppression, but this treatment was not his wish. He wrote to the King:

> "Procure for the Indians that are coming under our

---

[23] Lester Edwards, *The Life and Voyages of Vespucci*, New York, New Amsterdam Books, 1903, pg 75

rule, the same rules and protections as those we have been speaking of here in Spain. These rules are to apply to those in power and those not in power equally. I want them to have the same protection like I have as if they were my own flesh."[24]

When England picked up the banner of missionary zeal, they also became the world's leading superpower. They lost it for the very same reason. Then came America's turn. America's star was the brightest of all because the Christian missionary zeal was coupled with the highest form of the law. We are now losing it for the very same reasons. History is repeating itself. America is exporting a different kind of oppression, but the chains are still heavy. We export economic oppression and control. Money is loaned to a central government. The government then uses the money to centralize its control. The end result is that the people are oppressed. Unless we repent of this great evil, our fall is inevitable. We must repent, and again couple biblical missionary zeal with the export of personal liberty and freedom based upon individual responsibility and justice. Then the American Star will yet rise and remain the highest pinnacle of the sky.

GOD'S PLAN FOR WORLD PEACE

"And many people shall go and say, Come ye, and let us go up to the mountain of the Lord, to the house of the God of Jacob; and he will teach us of his ways, and we will walk in his paths: for out of Zion shall go forth the law, and the word of the Lord from Jerusalem. And he shall judge among the nations, and shall rebuke many people: and they shall beat their swords into plowshares, and their spears into pruning hooks: nation shall not lift up sword against nation, neither shall they learn war any more."

-Isaiah 2:3-4

---

[24] Christopher Columbus, *Letters to King Ferdinand and Queen Isabel*, 1496 Raccolta Collection.

This is God's formula for world peace, the coupling of the word from Jerusalem (the Bible) with the law from Zion (America's Constitutional law based upon eternal principle). The failure of world peace is our failure to follow God's formula. When we follow God's formula, the promises are sure as the warmth of the rising sun, and just as bright.

The Lord will "judge among the nations and rebuke many people". When the teaching of the law (from America) and the word (from Jerusalem) are combined in purity, nation will not lift up the sword against nation anymore and implements of war will be converted into implements of harvest. Our nation was founded by people who recognized this awesome blessing and responsibility. America's beacon light has been recognized as God's beacon light.

Jefferson view of a purpose of the revolution

Jefferson proposed that our nation's seal be God, leading the children of Israel following the pillar of fire.[25] Jefferson believed the Founding Fathers were trying to establish the principles of God's law in America so there could be a restoration of ancient Christianity upon this continent.

He said:

> "If the freedom of religion guaranteed us by law in theory can ever rise in practice under the overbearing inquisition of public opinion, truth will prevail over fanaticism, and the genuine doctrines of Jesus, so long perverted by his pseudo-priests, will again be restored to their original purity. This reformation will advance with the other improvements of the human mind, but too late for me to witness it."[26]

---

[25] W. Cleon Skousen, *The Making of America*, The National Center for Constitutional studies, Washington DC (no date given) pg 32-33

[26] Thomas Jefferson to Jared Sparks (4 Nov. 1820) as quoted in *The Real Thomas Jefferson* Part I by Andrew M. Allison National Center for Constitutional Studies, Washington DC, 1981, pg. 301

This appears to be on his mind at this time (1820) because he also wrote to another friend, F.A. Van Der Kemp,

"The genuine and simple religion of Jesus will one day be restored; such as was practiced by Himself"

If America's salt has lost its savor, it is henceforth good for nothing except to be cast out and trodden under the foot of men (Matthew 5:13). The time for us to repent has come.

CONCEPT SUMMARY

Our understanding of the law begins with recognition of the eternal and unchanging nature of God's law. Laws are threatened by man's pride that exalts himself to status of law maker or degenerates him to the level of a mob. In order for the law to be established we must first recognize the eternal nature of the law. Responsibility to the law must flow from the people upward, while accountability to the law is required from the government downward. Principle number five of just representation is a Republic based upon the great eternal laws.

CONCEPT NUMBER SIX
WORK AND GLORY

"But whoso looketh into the perfect law of liberty, and continueth therein, he being not a forgetful hearer, but a doer of the work, this man shall be blessed in his deed."

-James 1:25

There is a work necessary to precede glory. The spiritual revival of America precedes the revival of American strength and ideals. The heart of this revival is the restoration of the Republic based upon justice and responsibility, peace and independence, liberty and freedom. The sprit that moves this work is the spirit of God, our Father. Organization and a spirit of volunteerism can get the people back into politics and return the government back to the people.

The laws of our great Republic were, and are yet going to be based upon God's laws. The glory of what America may become is hardly to be imagined. This glory was conceived in the hearts of pilgrim refugees fleeing into the wilderness with hope of establishing the Kingdom of God on Earth.

This glory was born in 1776 in the blood and labor of an independent nation. It grew as America grew with work and labor of pioneers expanding the borders physically, economically, technologically, spiritually, intellectually, and morally. It matured to stand as the strongest and most able nation on Earth. Part of America died spiritually when we forsook the God of Heaven for the modern gods of socialism and humanism, greed and indulgence, dependency and control, injustice and materialism. America can be spiritually born again in the fiery baptism of repentance, and given the wings of eagles to soar to new and even greater heights.

The Independence Movement begins in the hearts of our people and changes the very soul of our country. The sickness in the head will find its strongest medicine in that remedy which first heals its heart. You are the heart. Healing begins with you.

Something more powerful than "what is"

The Independence Movement replaces party politics, special interests, mob democracy, and money power with a more just method of choosing our leaders. The responsibility and power comes from the people upward, but the accountability must follow from the head downward. The Independence Movement quietly, peacefully, efficiently, and more representatively calls our best to be our leaders. The great Biblical promise that God will restore our judges as at the first and our counselors as at the beginning preceding our return to righteousness (Isaiah 1:26) is the blueprint for our action. George Washington was our first and last president called to serve instead of seeking office. After Washington, a different pattern of politics began. We have had some great presidents, but it has been in spite of party politics, not because of them. Something powerful is in the concept of a calling to serve. This call brings many people to work together. The many called can then choose its best and most qualified to put before the vote of the people. Advantage is given to the most qualified, unselfish, and unencumbered, instead of merely those who seem to want position the most. Many statesmen are motivated by the most pure, true, and holy principles to seek position to accomplish that which is best, but the burden of modern politics, which favors those who will promise the most because they are willing to take the most, is an unnecessary evil.

Choosing representation

We believe in the principle of representation; the delegation of authority to study, debate, and intelligently choose and make decisions in our behalf by elected representatives. The most difficult, time-consuming and important decision is first choosing who the representative is to be. If we choose good representation then inevitably we will have good government. If we recognize that the purpose of good government is to protect the rights of the people under the delegated authority of the rights

115

of self-defense, then the principles of just representation will make sense. If we believe that the purpose of government is to provide a playground for politicians to experiment with their pet theories of socialism, other people's lives, or to play real-life monopoly with plundered loot and the rights and privileges of the people, then we will have little sympathy for the principles of just representation.

A fatal flaw of current politics

Current American politics elects representatives based upon what they say. This is a fatal flaw of our system. In order to avoid the wolves in sheep's clothing, we need to follow Christ and judge representatives based upon the fruits of their lives (Matthew 7:15-20). This is a very difficult and time-consuming responsibility, especially for people who do not personally know the candidate. Great caution is necessary in judging. A true shepherd, a sheepherder, and even a wolf will love a flock, but they love it in different ways and for different reasons.

The fruits of living justly and wisely will be unmistakable. A checklist of these fruits is found in the Biblical qualifications of a bishop (both the Church and the Kingdom should be built upon the very same correct principles of leadership). Use this checklist in calling candidates to serve.

> "A bishop then must be blameless, the husband of one wife, vigilant, sober, of good behavior, given to hospitality apt to teach;
> "Not given to wine, no striker, not greedy of filthy lucre; but patient, not a brawler, not covetous;
> "One that ruleth well his own house, having his children in subjection with all gravity;
> "(For if a man know not how to rule his own house, how shall he take care of the church of God?)
> "Not a novice, lest being lifted up with pride he fall into the condemnation of the devil.
> "Moreover he must have a good report of them

116

which are without; lest he fall into reproach and the snare of the devil."

(1 Timothy 3:2-7)

In our current political system, we often make our political choices based upon short sound bites or carefully orchestrated professionally tweaked video clips that may or may not be representative of the candidate's life. We want to make our judgments based on the fruits of the candidate's whole life, not just the briefest and shallowest propaganda.

Media and news spin

Just as it is dangerous to judge a candidate by paid advertisements, the media treatment of candidates can be just as ludicrous. We live in a time when the bias of our media (in general) is astonishing. We see good candidates maligned for their goodness. We also see much effort to "spin" the news to protect the "guilty". We know that the media today is largely influenced by the unseen hand and power of money control, yet this is the very power that we wish to be protected against. Probably no other power or influence has been as valuable in the protection of our liberty as the power of the free press. Sadly, there has probably not been another influence so destructive to our system of freedom and liberty as the major press, bought and paid for by the liberal establishment elite. The press can be a wonderful watch dog. However, many people think they are being protected, but in are in reality facing an attack dog trained to aid in the assault against freedoms and liberty.

We cannot trust the modern media machine for the vital information we need to make the choices necessary in choosing good candidates. Neither can we trust the political machinery of modern political parties. The time is ripe for the Independence Movement and its system of just representation.

Every participant a candidate

You are called to serve. The Independence Movement

117

begins with you. Each and every participant in this movement becomes a candidate. From the many candidates a few will be chosen to actually run for office. By accepting this responsibility a unity of feeling and purpose will follow. We may be less critical and more helpful when each realizes it might be their turn next. Candidacy is a responsibility we should not pass on to others unless we are willing to shoulder it ourselves. As a candidate, everyone in the movement is expected to take the oath of office to uphold the Constitution of the United States before beginning to participate, not just after the prize is won and the spoils are being eyed. A candidate should be evaluated early by the way they are actually living, rather than expecting "the leopard to change his spots" after the responsibility is transferred.

Training the individual through participation and service

The Independence Movement's power begins with individuals trained and committed to value independence and sovereignty. We must be responsible enough to value and protect rights of oneself and neighbors, and expose the activities of those who profess to love liberty, but inwardly are committed to its destruction. Liberty and a system of plunder are not compatible. The Independence Movement is to be built upon the principles of the Constitution and truths of justice from the ground up. The call is issued to the many from which we choose the few. This is a Biblical concept.

This author is indebted to Dr. Cleon Skousen whose writings, teachings, and personal mentoring originally brought these concepts to his attention. These principles are expounded upon in Dr. Skousen's excellent books, *The Making of America, The Substance* and *Meaning of the Constitution*, and *The Majesty of God's Law; It's Coming to America and The 5000 Year Leap.* The study of these three volumes will prove an excellent background, study, and reference, for any one interested in good government, just representation, the principles of God's law, and the United States Constitution.

Ancient Biblical principles were practiced politically by the Anglo-Saxons

These principles represent the most effective and fair system of choosing just representation ever devised. Dr. Skousen states:

> "Jefferson had already discovered the basic pattern for a model constitution by studying two ancient peoples who had both lived under People's Law. He had found that ancient Israel was the first nation in history to have a system of representative government; then he discovered that 1,500 years later the Anglo-Saxons were living under a system which was almost identical. Both Franklin and Jefferson later wrote that these people were the source of the 'ancient principles' which were the 'wisest and most perfect ever yet devised by the wit of man.'
>
> "Jefferson was quoted as stating that it was from the Anglo-Saxons that 'we claim the honor of being descended whose political principles and form of government we have assumed.' "[27]

The beauty of just representation is that candidates are called to serve instead of seeking office

This is an extremely powerful, nation-altering concept. Instead of reforming our very corrupt campaigning practices, it replaces it with something more fair, just, and efficient. Wealth or debt is no longer necessary to purchase the office through media and advertising. The information necessary is inexpensively, and in a much more unbiased fashion, carried to each interested voter. Through a system the voter helped create, information is both given and received.

---

[27] W. Cleon Skousen, *The Making of America, the Substance and Meaning of the Constitution* pg.47, 48

Using the system within our current election procedures

The system is incorporated within the framework of our current election procedures by becoming a candidate selection mechanism. The process still utilizes the popular vote of the people to ratify the selection of candidates through the established election procedures. America has always been about choices. The Independence Movement gives the voters an alternative in their selection process. The Independence Movement in no way interferes with candidates also being offered through the established political system. It does, however, give a choice to those interested in real political change and reform.

Look at the historical functioning of principles as established Biblically under Moses and as also implemented by the Anglo-Saxons. Then examine opportunities to utilize these powerful concepts today

The Biblical model set up by Moses consisted first of individuals capable of governing themselves (individual sovereignty). At the broadest level, groups of ten families each were established. Then followed groups of fifty families, hundreds, and thousands. The people were instructed to "take" or choose wise understanding and known men as leaders over these groups (Deuteronomy 1:9-15). This organization existed under the Law of Moses.

This same basis of government was followed by the Anglo-Saxons. Good King Alfred (877 to 899 AD), who was both a Christian and an Anglo-Saxon, said "This law was first revealed in the Hebrew tongue".[28] King Alfred wrote the concepts of Anglo-Saxon laws in his native language. Thomas Jefferson was so impressed with these concepts that he actually learned the Anglo-Saxon language that he might study them as originally written. Jefferson sent copies of his translation to his friends. Later, he proposed that one side of the great seal of the

---

[28] Sharon Turner, *The History of the Anglo Saxons,* London, Longman Reese 1936 as quoted in *The Majesty of God's Law* pg.298

United States have a representation of Hengist and Horsa, the Saxon chiefs who first entered England about AD 450.

Under the Anglo-Saxon system, this head of ten families was called a tithing man. 50 families organized into a vill or village. The one hundred families had a hundred man, and 1,000 families was a shire with an eolderman (shortened to earl) assisted by a "shire reef" (sheriff).[29]

The beauty of this organization is the effectiveness of responsibility going up and accountability coming down to the people

In times of crisis, need, disaster, or even the death or removal of leaders, the people were organized in such a way that the voice of the people could be heard, organization reestablished, and unity of action accomplished. The people were organized at the smallest level to protect their individual sovereignty, establish justice, and choose the best and most capable people which they were intimately acquainted with to represent them in the difficult and time-consuming job of choosing leaders. Thus, an in-depth study of the candidates was accomplished through delegation of the responsibility to their wisest, most intelligent, and best neighbors. Each person could express their worries, fears, needs, and expectations to a personal representative and expect feedback in return. This system is much more participatory than what we currently have. This fosters civic and individual responsibility, and political awareness, it amounts to just and accountable representation. The system also trains, through service, future citizen-statesmen.

Added Value to Voters

Imagine how refreshing it will be to see candidates offered upon ballots that have not "polluted" themselves through campaigning, promising, and fund raising. Imagine the added value to our people knowing that the candidates offered through

---

[29] W. Cleon Skousen, *The Making of America,* pg.54, 55

the Independence Movement will not spend time, money, or effort worrying about, or actually engaged in the process of campaigning towards election or re-election. It is believed that election, or re-election, efforts consumes 20-50% of most politicians' time. The Independence Movement will make this waste obsolete. Imagine how the leadership of the Independence Movement can revolutionize politics and purify political corruption and waste.

When a candidate for the Independence Movement appears on the ballet, the voters may not be as informed through campaigning and paid promotions, but will have available much more of the pertinent information about the candidate from what is expected to be a more reliable source. In our current age of information, quantity of information is not as much of a problem as the source, and the reliability of the information. Knowing that the candidate was "called to serve" by this representational form of selection may give this candidate an edge. The voters also know this candidate will be closely watched and monitored during office by this same organization.

Representatives of the Independence Movement will be in a much better position to personally evaluate the qualifications of a candidate in depth. More scrutiny of the candidate can be given than through the current system. The representatives that issue calls to serve will know that their evaluation represents the delegated responsibility of many people. Very in-depth evaluation is encouraged. This is in addition to the final scrutinizing given by individual voters on election day.

Value to candidates

In addition to what this system of just representation does to call the best to serve and give us higher quality candidates, look at what the system does for those who are called to serve. The candidate is freed from the distasteful need to campaign, beg for money, commit personal fortunes, or seek the favors of the rich, powerful, or established, to be a serious contender. Many part time volunteer hours would be far more effective than a few full time professional campaigners with special interest money.

Modern campaigning is a bare-knuckled, lawless, no holds barred, financial fist fight. It favors those who can beg, borrow, steal, or personally commit the most. The system wounds, or financially destroys, both winner and loser. The saddest part of this wasteful spectacle is that often there is little relevance between campaign fighting skills and those skills most needed to fulfill the responsibility. If we would not want to be subjected to a financial whipping and fight, why should we expect this of our political leaders (judges)?

We expect the bypassed influences (financial controllers and influence brokers) to seek to discredit this movement and its candidates. Efforts by the establishment to discredit the movement will be a measure of the system's effectiveness. This system is not reliant upon money to function and has its own information dissemination organization. This movement should be able to function in spite of the wailing and winds of established power.

Most people are disgusted over our current political realities. The Independence Movement is expected to glean the force of a massive grass root's power wave. People feel disenfranchised by modern politics and are expected to fill the ranks of this new political force. This is a movement whose time has come. The Independence Movement will foster a great return to the underlying principles of justice. This return to justice is a return to God, who is its author. The key to the movement's success is you.

Getting Started

The Independence Movement will start with concerned citizens building organizations that will make the movement eligible to put candidates upon the ballot in city, county, state, or national elections. Individuals will contact their neighbors to inform and create basic units. The rights and responsibilities of the individual must above all be remembered, fostered and protected. This is the Independence Movement.

Power stems from the strength of individuals committed to living justly and to the work of building. Mobs may destroy, committees may debate, despots may plunder, but there is nothing so powerful as a society of individuals cooperating in the work of building, lifting, enlightening, and sharing in the rewards of a just and free society. History is full of examples of the power of grass roots movements. Everyone wants to feel that they are a part something important. The cause, the call and the work, accompanied with a spiritual conformation and divine blessing become an unstoppable unification force. Responsibility to protect individual rights starts with the individual.

The answer starts with accepting and valuing freedom, independence, and responsibilities. This makes peace possible. Our own families must be established upon the principles of justice and the blessings of peace and liberty. These blessings are extended to the neighborhood, the community, the state, and the nation. When we cease to tolerate injustice and plunder, we will cease to be robbed and victimized. When an injustice to any is an affront upon all, great will be the peace and the liberty of our people. When we strengthen our homes and families, we strengthen our nation. When we become converted within our hearts to the principles of equality and justice, our nation will be transformed into a Mecca of freedom and liberty.

The defense of our nation begins with the defense of personal rights and responsibilities. Real personal security comes from personal integrity and strength. The internal weakness of a society, enslaved in dependency and control, will eventually crumble and fall in upon itself. This is a historical reality. It is also true that a people who believe that resistance to tyranny is a service to God cannot be long enslaved. The individual responsibilities of self-defense are the basis of all liberty. The personal commitment to resist tyranny, while building upon the principles of freedom and liberty, are the work and goal of the Independence Movement.

THOUGHTS ON SELF-DEFENSE

To stand on hallowed ground, made sacred by the sacrifice and blood of the great patriots who have preceded us, is to also feel the importance of the work we now face. Every man or woman who has ever stood up to face tyranny has realized that the space they occupied, they alone can defend. Each of us has our own part, our own space, and our own responsibilities. Each of us must be willing to stand in defense of that which is most precious and sacred. What we do must be motivated by love.

Our legacy is that we have been given the rights of freedom and the power to maintain that freedom within the peace of a just society. We must use eternal vigilance to maintain that freedom and liberty with every peaceful means, but never, never, never surrender our right to stand, even alone if need be, in defense of our natural rights.

We first defend our rights, then conquer injustice, and then we build.

I have stood on Concord Bridge. Soil once absorbed the worthy blood of those who realized that, in their then-and-now, it really did depend all upon them. What is it that makes a person stand when every instinct, reason, and fear would shout retreat? Let someone else fill the breach, bear the cross, or carry the burden. These are natural thoughts, but something divine raises average ordinary people to do the great, the eternal, and the lasting.

On one fourth of July, an overwhelming feeling of gratitude and love for America was upon me. Words of the following poem seemed to write themselves as they were penned. May we all rise up individually to the challenges before us and never lose sight of what it has taken to bring us this far. We must defend our rights at all cost. We must shoulder our responsibility with all diligence. We must never allow our responsibilities or rights to be voted, usurped, or taken away.

This poem expresses some feelings about the rights and responsibilities of self-defense

30 PACES
By Farley Anderson

Thirty paces of hallowed ground
Did separate the foe.
An icy chill swept o'er their blood
As they wondered who would go.
The men in red paid by the crown
On orders to fulfill
Or men in plain, armed with the truth,
On freedom's side so still.

Each side did have their reasons
For being there that day
And what they did at freedom's door
Would show the future's way-
The men in red were coming
To take the free men's guns
The men in plain were standing
For their rights as freedom's sons.

We'll have no king, but our true God,
By whose love we are bought
Or force and chains will bow us down
To a tyrant's will, un-fought.
The last vote of the people
Is a free man's call to arms
Yet the tyrant sees no need of this
"For he'll keep us from all harms."

Unless we wish to keep our gold
Or assert our rights from our God.
Or differ in the way we think
Or walk on freedom's sod.
The years have come and they have gone
Yet, things remain the same

As here we stand at freedom's door
Yet called by freedom's name.

History yet remembers
Concord and Lexington
And the shot heard 'round the world
As they came to take their gun.
Wherever free men gather
They know this message true
That never was a people free
Without the means to follow through.

Perhaps what we now call a right
Should be a responsibility
And every man should do his part
To keep our nation free.
A right received from Father
Is such a sacred thing
That what is lost by compromise
His wrath to us doth bring.

Just 30 steps between us
If we bow, then all is lost
And future will be sacrificed
And infinite the cost
The tyrants, they are standing
With their coats all drenched in blood.
And walk upon the graves and lives
They swept away by flood.

"Just step aside a little
And trust your soul to us
And go to sleep in secure bliss
And stop this silly fuss.
How can you hope to stand alone
Against our army great

And overcome our marching force
That's driven by our hate."

Oh, deep within the free man's soul
Is the warmth of freedom's light.
And the sure knowledge-we're not alone
And this is God's own fight.
For if we stand on freedom's sod
We never stand alone
And even if our lives are lost
His Kingdom is our home.

You'll never take our arms from us
While life within us flows
And this last vote we vow to keep
A tyrant to dispose.
For many who gave up this right
Found out when just too late
That 30 steps, swing open or close,
Upon this freedom's gate.

CONCEPT SUMMARY

The organization of the Independence Movement is based upon individual strength, family strength, neighborhood strength, community strength, state strength, and national strength. These are the fortified defense bastions of a free society. The restoration of our Republic is the glory sought. The sixth principle of just representation is work. If we are to receive God's glory, it must be preceded by doing God's work. The work ahead is to restore our Republic. We must overcome party politics, special interests, mob democracy, and money power, to reestablish freedom and liberty in America.

"To this end we pledge our lives, our fortunes, and our sacred honor."

So help us, God.

BOOK SUMMATION

The Independence Movement, to restore freedom and liberty through a restoration of our Republic, is centered upon principles of just representation. Modern politics is a mixture of wheat and tares growing together. As America matures, the need to separate from the choking influences of special interests, party politics, mob democracy, and money power is apparent. A restoration can occur when we are represented by our best and most capable statesmen. We need leaders called to judge according to the principles of justice.

So much of our strength, power and goodness are being squandered upon that which is incapable of yielding fruit. Non-productive influences are so intermingled with the productive, that the true cost of their choking has been camouflaged. As good people gravitate towards correct principles and just representation, power, growth, and strength will be magnified. The fruits of freedom and liberty will be reestablished upon the yet-fertile soil of America.

With this hope the great Godly promises are sought. We return to the correct principles that restore our nation's judges as at the first (Isaiah 1:26). A profound national and world peace is expected as the word and the law is combined in the hearts of the people (Isaiah 2:2-4). As people look up, they will begin to see the long awaited marriage of Heavenly principles and Earthly government (Revelation 19:7-8) (Matthew 6:10).

Hope precedes faith, motivating us to action. We seek to establish a system that first calls our best people to serve and then provides the tools to see the process successfully through to election and service.

Limited government protects the rights and responsibilities of a self-governing and righteous people. The blessings of Heaven will sweep across our nation like a flood as this work is accomplished. As people return to God, the power and blessings of God will return to us. Recognizing the eternal nature of just law is the beginning. Delegation of power by law (the basis of our Republic) flows from the people upward, while accountability to the law is required from the government downward.

This movement is a second great American Revolution. The seeds of this movement are planted within your heart where it will grow as you grow. Its power will be your power, its glory your glory, its success your success.

This is something bigger than ourselves. As we lose ourselves in the cause of right, we may just discover who we really are. Like the first American Revolution, this movement is not about greed, lust, favors, or the love of power, but about our birthright of freedom, liberty, and the power of love.

The light of this movement is shining from above to brighten the dawn of a new millennium. To see the sun rise from a templed peak of a mountain height requires sacrifice, dedication, intelligence, honor, justice, love, and work. From the exalted peaks, American patriots will echo the proclamation of liberty that will be heard throughout the land.

HOW TO BEGIN
METHODS AND STRUCTURE

This section contains suggestions of how the process might work. Innovation, use, practicality, and necessity will modify, update, or replace parts of the process over time. How the work is structured is less important than the return to God and correct principles. The call to serve answered by many individuals and, ultimately, by our political leaders is also more important. Yet, this must have structure for it to have meaning.

Simply stated, the Independence Movement's purpose is to organize so that we can:

A. Set higher standards of political morality, and help

each other learn, teach, understand, and incorporate correct leadership principles.

B. Create and utilize a simple system to choose from among our ranks and call to serve the most honorable and best qualified to enter the political arena.

C. Build and strengthen the organization so that power is shifted away from party politics, special interests, mob democracy, and money power, and back towards the responsibility of the people.

D. Support publicly-elected officials in the discharge of their duty and give citizen input in an organized, effective and timely manner. Through this service, raise statesmen.

E. Evaluate the electorate in terms of freedom and liberty, as judged by set standards of accountability. Give clout to this evaluation by means of unity of action and the ability to distribute information.

In looking at any new structure, great care must be used to not end up with different means to the same end or even something worse. The pridefulness of secret agendas, or the combining of evil, are the natural enemies to open and fair governing and must be detected early and diligently guarded against. Selfishness must be removed from government from the bottom up. If we do not begin with ourselves, then we will be receiving the government we deserve. If we do start with our self, we can, with faith, call upon God to raise up to us righteous leaders, even if our structure is not perfect at first.

We expect success because:
1. Correct principles in action are more powerful than party politics

2. Citizens organized in a great cause are more powerful than special interests.

3. Understanding the principles of our Nation "as at the first" is more powerful than mob democracy.

4. The call to serve, answered by many citizens, is more powerful than money power.

5. The power and unity of the movement can continue to build over time, giving advantage to its candidates.

6. God, the author of our liberty, is waiting to be called upon in faith. This is more powerful than anything. We expect miracles.

Ideas for starting with a temporary state organization

A temporary state organization may be necessary to get things started and could be created by dividing a state into ten sections. In each section, concerned citizens could be encouraged to gather for instruction and to put these principles into action. It is vital that whenever people are brought together to receive instruction and participate, that planning and organization is sufficient that time is not wasted, confusion is minimized, and results are apparent. A meaningful purpose, correct principles, structure, participation, and follow-through, are the keys. These should be apparent to everyone in order to avoid being sidetracked by hidden agendas or lost to confusion. A simple organization to select a representative to send to the state level is the first task. An easy way this could be accomplished is to simply divide into groups of approximately ten, (more or less depending on total number of participants so that the end group will be close to ten) based upon the neighborhood proximity of participant's homes. A head count of all participants is taken. Head counts of participants must be accurate and verified as there may be a time where a weighted vote is the most fair or desirable way to assure representation. Each group of approximately ten each (by neighborhood proximity) then breaks to choose and call a representative. This representative moves up a level and this process of creating groups of ten is repeated until one area representative is chosen to go to the state level to help organize and facilitate the work necessary at the state level to start to accomplish the movement's objectives. It would be unusual for the size of the group to be exactly divisible by ten so the actual groups would probably be in number from five to fifteen.

An organization is left in place with no one being required to contact more than approximately 10 people to get any message back to each participant. Each participant also has a method to give input going all the way up to the top. This initial structure, created to start the ball rolling, may be disbanded as soon as its objectives are met.

Objectives might include the following:

1. Calendar—Create a calendar to coordinate effort.
2. Party relations—Explore which party, or parties, are compatible with the movement's objectives and procedures or if a new party is necessary.
3. Information—Create an information network.
4. Treasury—Organize a treasury.
5. Teaching—Teach and disseminate the movement's principles and public relations.
6. National—Make plans to tie into or create a national organization.
7. Candidate selection—Make plans to help put a movement representative on the ballet of every possible election by supporting regional organizations.
8. Other objectives as they become apparent.
9. Chairing coordination of the entire group.
10. Vice-chairing to support chairing.

Each one of the delegates could assume one of these responsibilities. Responsibilities could be rearranged as needed or work-load dictated.

After the initial organization phase and the candidate

selection process begin, the state organizing group could be replaced with a group to issue the call to the highest state office for that year. The candidate selection process could be very similar to that used to create a state organization. A meeting of concerned citizens (potential candidates) could be called. The oath of office should be administered to everyone involved. The same methods may again be used. The idea is that all organization starts at the neighborhood level with groups of approximately ten who choose a representative to go on to the next level. The process is repeated until only one group of approximately ten is left. This last remaining group is the one that deliberates to issues the call and stays in place for as long as its choice of candidate has a term of office. For a state position, a region or county could send a delegate to create a committee of ten at the state level. If it becomes too difficult to choose between several good choices it appears that it is Biblically sanctioned to cast lots, thus in theory reserving the judgment unto God. This does not, however, remove the responsibility each of us has to work and study to make righteous judgments, or the opportunity to seek divine inspiration.

The group of ten, who issues the call to serve, is responsible to describe the reasons for the calling of this person so that all who participate can feel good about the choice. Since the Independence Movement does not allow for its candidates to be encumbered with campaign debt, spend their own money, or seek the help of special interest groups, it becomes the work of everyone involved in the movement to take the information to the voters. Voters must be able to see the advantages of supporting leaders that were called to serve by a citizen support group. Information to make a wise choice is supplied to voters and reasons why they will not be seeing the typical campaigning is explained by their friends and neighbors working in service to show the better way. This can be more powerful than paid promotions or current campaigning practices. Of course, we should seek exposure of the candidates to the voters in ways that do not involve paid advertising and campaigning. It is acceptable for the Independence Movement to campaign on behalf of its candidates, but we want to avoid those who are promoting themselves. The bottom line is that everyone who helps in the issuing of the call should also be committed to the process of seeing it through to election. This means work. This work can replace all or most all of the money currently spent on elections.

The committee of the ten issuing the call to the candidate to serve remains in place as long as the candidate remains in office, and until a new committee is chosen to either reissue the call to serve to the incumbent or to call a new representative to be a candidate for office. The duties of the committee are to keep the citizens informed via the organizations information network, counsel, and issue recommendations on behalf of the organization, and at the end of the service term, report on the candidate's term of office in respect to service rendered. This would include constitutionality, preservation of freedom and liberty, special challenges, fiscal responsibility, etc. On the national level, each state could select a single delegate to form a national council for the purpose of issuing a call for a presidential candidate. Since the number of participants in the movement would vary from state to state, each delegate could carry a weighted vote in respect to the number of members of the Independence Movement represented. This national council would also be responsible to direct and co-ordinate the movement and support the candidates on the national level. In general, it really can be this simple. Never underestimate the power of good people working together towards great objectives.

How Do We Spread the Message?
We change the political face of America by starting with our own heart, our own home, and our own neighborhood. There are good people that you know. There are good people where you live and work. Your calling is to help where you are. The Independence Movement begins with you.

Imagine introducing friends, family and acquaintances to this challenge. Do not be afraid to ask for help to change the way we put our candidates on the ballot. Explain that this is how we can restore our political leaders (judges) as at the first (Isaiah 1:26) to claim the promised blessings. This is how to put statesmen above the politicians and remove the wolves in sheep's clothing. (Matthew 7:15-16, 20). Explain how the movement seeks to reestablish freedom and liberty through citizen responsibility and just representation. Help others see that help is needed so that our candidate can be elected without creating conflicting obligations to party politics, special interests, mob democracy, or money power. Point out that we now have an alternative to what "has been" for so long.

All should be able to see the added value of voting for a candidate who will not be spending time, money, effort, or creating obligations through the campaigning process. We need candidates whose loyalty is to the law and to the people. Show how a profile created in the process of issuing the call is more valid and helpful in choosing the best candidate for leadership than the promises or propaganda we have been used to. Explain that every person who wishes to be involved in issuing the call also becomes a candidate. The commitment by each person, along with the oath of office taken by everyone in the movement is part of the movement's power and meaning. Explain the difference between more and more promises and true representation used to protect justice and the law.

Help spread the word.

Help make the movement meaningful.

Help restore the judges as at the first.

Help save our Republic.

A Last Parting Thought

The author of this book once had a dream that seemed to be full of meaning.

There was a large hall filled with many people anxiously walking past. Every attempt to deliver a message of hope and warning was met with complete indifference, as the people simply continued on, looking neither to the right or left. This went on for an extended period of time.

The next impression was that of being at a speaker's platform in front of the whole group. After looking around, it was apparent that no text for the speech was provided. Even more startling was a large screen behind the podium where a picture was projected that was meant to be used as the subject of the speech. The image was that of a popular nursery rhyme. A pause to earnestly plead for divine guidance was answered by a calm assurance. Not knowing what to say, the speech was simply begun.

"Rub a dub-dub. Three men in a tub, and who do you think they be? The butcher, the baker, the candlestick maker, turn them out, knaves all three." We learn some very important things as small children and this children's rhyme contains some very important advice, "Turn them out, knaves all three."

Who is represented here? On the right, we have the butcher. He is covered in blood. Like Cain before him, he is the keeper of the great secret that in this temporary Earthly situation, murder is profitable. I continued to explain that in the book of Revelation, we read of the great last-day whore drunk with the blood of saints and martyrs of Jesus. We see revolutionaries, profiteers, and criminals who kill for profit. So many of those murdered by the communists, socialists, Nazi's, political corrupters, etc. die not so much because their ideology is so offensive, but rather because these systems need plunder to survive and murder facilitates plunder.

On the other side of the tub, we see the candlestick maker. He represents the false light from the great man-made gods of the last days. The philosophies include those of the great false prophet, Karl Marx, whose doctrines have led to the murder of one hundred million souls during the last century and the internal weakening

137

of law and order. The Marxist doctrine encompasses the communistic, socialistic, humanistic, NAZI (National Socialist Worker's Party) and other false and damning doctrines used to replace the true light.

In the center of the picture, between the other two characters, is the baker. He represents those with the dough. Consider all the evil brought and bought into the world because we have allowed our monetary system to be usurped. The love of money is the root of all evil and central to this picture, because the gold and silver and treasures of the Earth have been the enabling factor for all other evil. Remove satanic control of the dough (money) and the butcher and the candlestick maker become much less significant. The seventeenth chapter of Revelation is the story of the breaking of the marriage covenant between our people and our government. Like fornication, it began with a banker's boast that our government could operate on borrowed and fiat money, without direct accountability to the people. As with fornication, it felt good for a while, but then we see an evil entity ending up ruling over the kings of the Earth. This plunder has been used to finance every form of evil, every act of corruption, every tyranny, and every war, and (most insidiously) the propagation of false ideology.

I concluded by saying we see all three types combined in one tub, trying to make themselves look respectable. His Kingdom come, His will be done, on Earth as it is in Heaven, is not possible while this great combination of evil sits enthroned. We must recognize the knaves for what they are and turn them out, all three types, from our personal lives, our families, our communities, states, nation, and the world.

At this conclusion, I found myself wide awake. After pondering the significant meaning I got up and recorded the dream.

Appendix A: Political Exposé from the Book of Revelation

The book of Revelation may be the most important political documentary available for our day. John's message may have the power to unite believers of many faiths. John describes six evil satanic entities on Earth in the last days. If we look at the descriptions, what the entities are doing, and are not afraid to look at things politically, we may begin to see. These evil entities are set up here on Earth, and as a result, the Earth goes through seven last-day plagues. The effect, apparently, is the destroying of these entities in reverse order of their introduction in the book of Revelation, and preparing the Earth for the Marriage Supper of the Lamb. A message of the Book of Revelation is, "Come out of her, my people, that ye be not partakers of her sins, and that ye receive not of her plagues" (Revelation 17:4). Christ comes to a prepared people. (Revelation 19:7, 8) These six entities appear to be:

1. Satan and his angels cast to earth, working through the following five entities:
2. Communism or the red beast, the military superpower that leaves bear tracks and is the destroyer of the whore after its own pseudo death
3. The United Nations, which is another beast, a world wide organization, voice for communism and socialism, deceiver of the world
4. Socialism, the image of communism, an economic system that numbers and marks everyone as its slave
5. Unclean spirits like three frogs, subversive workers above and below the surface to world leaders, representatives of communism, Marxist doctrine and Satan bringing the world to war
6. International controllers of the world banking system, the great whore, mystery workers, deceivers and controllers of world leaders, destroyers of silver coin, diluters of money, controllers of communists, drunk with the blood of martyrs. Let us begin our analysis.

The **_first_** of the six satanic entities is Satan himself, along with his organization and his followers called his angels (Revelation

139

12:9), revealed as the "red dragon" (Revelation 12:3). We note with interest that the "old serpent, called the Devil and Satan" (Revelation 12:9), was known as red even before being cast out of heaven (Revelation 12:3). Importantly, Revelation 12:10 points out that salvation, strength, and the kingdom of our God was pronounced in heaven only after the accuser was cast out. Making accusations is a method used by many today in order to gain power.

We learn from verse 11 of this chapter what it takes to overcome this evil:

1. The blood of the Lamb
2. The word of their testimonies
3. A love of higher principles that exceeds even the love of their own lives

(Revelation 12:11)

These are needed for overcoming evil today.

Satan was cast out of heaven and came to this earth (Revelation 12:9) because his plan, motives, and character were incompatible with the order of heaven. A terrible war is now being waged for the souls of mankind. The battleground is this earth (Revelation 12:12), the stakes are eternal glory, and the good guys win. This is the great underlying message of hope from the Book of Revelation. Satan is revealed as he which deceiveth the whole world (Revelation 12:9). This is also the goal of the earthly conspirators. Naturally, the truth is the greatest weapon against such satanic deception. We now move beyond the dragon, to understand his earthly method of operation.

John begins working from the most obvious to that which is most mysterious. This is also how most of us approach the problem of trying to educate those around us of the global conspiracy to rob our freedom.

The **second** entity is the beast. Let us compare the beast with communism. The descriptive features of the beast are found in Revelation chapters 13 and 17. The beast has seven heads which are seven great satanic kingdoms of the world which have usurped mankind's unalienable rights (Revelation 12:3, and the interpretation from Revelation 17:10-12). In John's day, five of the satanic kingdoms had already fallen. At that time, one existed (the corrupted Roman Empire) and the last (coming in the last days) is not yet come. These same kingdoms are the subject of King Nebuchadnezzar's dream which was interpreted by Daniel the Prophet (Daniel 2).

The beast is like unto a leopard (Revelation 13:2). Leopards are creatures of the night, of shadows and darkness. The most often seen evidence of their existence are the carcasses left behind. This analogy fits with communism. Nations and kingdoms are enslaved while one hundred million people have been murdered this past century by the communists. This beast has the feet of a bear (Revelation 13:2) and thus leaves bear tracks. Politically speaking, the bear tracks of today lead back to the Russian bear, the first communist country of our era. The beast has the mouth of a lion. This may be a little more difficult to understand, but consider Karl Marx, the false prophet and mouth for communism. Karl Marx after leaving Germany lived in England, which uses the banner of the lion. He was born of Jewish ancestry, which also uses the banner of the lion. On both of these accounts, Marx was not true to his heritage. He denied the heritage of the great English statesmen, and he was not true to the special calling of being a keeper and representative of the principles of God's divine law as revealed to Moses. A lion could also be indicative of power to rule and a predatory nature.

In Revelation 13:3 we see an unmistakable feature of the beast that should be recognized by all today. The beast is wounded in the head unto death, but is not really killed. This important warning (that communism's death is not a reality) is repeated five times in the Book of Revelation (Revelation 13:3, 13:12, 13:14, 17:8, 17:11). We next see that the beast is a military superpower (Revelation 13:4). From Revelation 13:8 we learn that almost all the earth shall worship the beast. The word *worship* is strong, but consider the way the doctrines of communism are taught and learned, and the way, directly and indirectly, the world financially supports communism. We then realize that the word *worship* is very appropriately used. Last, but not least, we see in Revelation 17:3 that the beast is scarlet colored. Identifying the beast as satanic communism may be as simple as asking who the reds are. Lucifer used red as his banner in the pre-mortal world. The marxist followers of our day are likewise known as Red communists or socialists.

Next we see the beast (which is communism) is given a mouth (a voice), speaking great things and blasphemies (Revelation 13:5). This leads us to the ***third*** satanic entity known as another beast (Revelation 13:11). Compare the relationship between the beast and the second beast with the relationship of communism to the United Nations. Calling the United Nations a mouth for communism is a fitting description. When the average person thinks of the United Nations, he thinks of a place where there is excessive speeches and rhetoric. This is also how the Revelator begins his understanding of the other beast. It is a mouth for communism (Revelation 13:5) speaking great things and blasphemies. Its mouth is against God (Revelation 13:6). It spake as a dragon (Revelation 13:11). It causeth the earth (it is worldwide) and them which dwell therein to worship (support financially and learn and teach the doctrines) of the first beast (Revelation 13:12). It deceiveth them that dwell on the earth (Revelation 13:14).

The focus toward the United Nations is sharpened in Revelations 13:11. The other beast comes out of the earth, teaching that it is a world organization. The other beast has two horns (Revelation 13:11). The earth surrounded by two horns like a lamb is even a good description of the UN logo. Further in Revelation 17:12 we see that horns are kings (worldly powers). The United Nations' power is separated into two divisions of power, NATO and the Warsaw Pact. The horns are also indicative of being armed, but armed like a lamb? The United Nations does not send out soldiers, but rather "peacekeepers" and is thus armed like a lamb. By outward observation it would appear that the two horns (NATO and the Warsaw Pact) are warring against each other. Only when we consider that the stated objective of the United Nations is to politically unite all nations, do we see that these wars are actually furthering the goals of this second beast. The second beast exercises all the power of the first beast before him (Revelation 13:12). Likewise, the doctrines of the United Nations are in harmony with the global objectives of communism, and the U.N. was established after communism.

To the supporters of this movement, the scripture gives this warning: "He that leadeth into captivity shall go into captivity; he that killeth with the sword must be killed with the sword" (Revelation 13:10).

To complete our understanding of the other beast, which is the United Nations, John gives the description of an actual world event. It is a media event, done on the earth in the sight of men (Revelation 13:13). Its purpose was to "deceiveth them that dwell on the earth" (Revelation 13:14). Let us consider the first Gulf War. To do something in the sight of men in our day must surely mean putting it on TV. Never was a war so widely covered by the media. This was the first time our military was completely under the leadership of the United Nations, and so tying this event to the other beast fits. He doeth great wonders (Revelation 13:13). Again this is a fitting description of the Gulf War. Then comes the clincher: "he maketh fire come down from heaven on the earth in the sight of men" (Revelation 13:13). Many of us recall TV images of scud missiles being brought down from heaven in flames as they were destroyed by patriot missiles. Remember newsmen describing this as the miracle of being able to hit a bullet with a bullet? John the Revelator uses the same language (Revelation 13:14). This event is also done in the sight of the beast, fitting with the actual event which was watched by the communists, but not directly participated in by them (Revelation 13:14)

We have become aware, long after the war, that our patriot missiles at that time were not nearly as effective nor miraculous as we were led to believe on television. Our media is able to shape events and our perception through its single and directed eye to further the objectives of those who produce the programs. We can contrast this with a true miracle occurring at the same time which was never reported in the western press.

In order to appease or get the support of his Arab neighbors, Saddam Hussein had stated that one of his major objectives was

143

the destruction of Israel. He claimed that he would be able to annihilate one half the population and had the scud missiles to back up that threat. Israel had been convinced to let the United Nations and United States protect them. They did not strike early to remove the threat as had been their effective strategy in the past. Israel was hit by 39 scud missiles in densely populated areas. The destruction was devastating (3,773 buildings damaged or destroyed, including 16,992 individual apartments and 1,235 private homes). The great miracle is that not a single person was killed. The President of Israel at the time, Chaim Herzog, in a national address said:

> The Jewish nation witnessed many miracles in its history, from the splitting of the Red Sea to this very day. This time, as well, we were blessed with Divine intervention.

IDF (Israel Defense Forces) senior general, Moshe Bar Kochba, in his postwar analysis included the following from his on-the-spot observation of the missile destruction:

> I speak as a military man and as a realist, and I clearly state that there is no way rationally to understand the wondrous events which we are beholding. These days even the most hardened military officers speak consistently of "miracles." Their logical explanations have run out. . . What we have here is a series of wonders . . . Layers of miracles upon miracles.

One miracle was done in the sight of men (on television); one was not even reported. The Lord promised that He would again recover his people Israel. This event is typical of God's power and what will occur in the future, if we have eyes to see. As we read the Book of Revelation, keep in mind that God is a God of miracles.

Having a lead into John's description of the **_fourth_** satanic entity, we are told that the other beast says to those dwelling on the earth that they should make an image to the beast (Revelation 13:14). If the beast is communism, then the image of the beast must surely be socialism. Let us see if the pieces of the puzzle fit. The ultimate end result of socialism and communism are identical: control of the people, means of production, and economy. Only the means to the end differ. The communists believe in revolution and force, while the socialists believe in the slow corruption of the laws and the people.

The first great push toward socialism, in modern history, was initiated in France by the supporters of the bloody French Revolution. From Revelation 20:4 we read "and I saw the souls of them that were beheaded for the witness of Jesus, and the word of God, and which had not worshiped the beast neither his image . . . and they lived and reigned with Christ a thousand years." The next great socialist experiment began with the National Socialist German Workers Party or NAZI as we all know it.

The other beast, or the United Nations as we are now seeing it, also has power to give life to the image of the beast (Revelation 13:15). It gives power to the image of the beast so it can speak, and it kills those who would not worship the image of the beast (Revelation 13:15).

How do we know the image of the beast is socialism? The image of the beast is an economic system that controls buying and selling (Revelation 13:17) and so is socialism. This system applies to all people (Revelation 13:16). Since all governments are now moving towards socialism, this fits. When the relationship between communism, the United Nations, and the image of the beast entity are considered, then socialism is the logical choice. Consider how under the socialistic welfare state everyone has been numbered. What began as a little freedom traded for a little security is revolving towards totalitarian control and the promise of absolute security. The curse of the Book of Revelation comes to those who both have the mark and worship his image (Revelation 14:11, 15:2, 19:20, 20:4-5). Has our allegiance and reliance upon God and individual responsibility and accountability to Him been usurped by our allegiance and reliance on the socialistic welfare state? A question to ask is why would the mark of the beast (communism) be brought up while we are being taught of the image of the beast (socialism)?

145

Could John the Revelator be teaching that the ends are the same? Once individual rights and freedom are lost, does it matter whether they fall all at once through revolution or were voted or usurped away one by one? Either way, the progression of God's children is stopped and the deceiver is enthroned (2 Thessalonians 2:4).

For a greater understanding of the mark of the beast, let us return to the symbolism of the letters 666 from the Greek text. The word *mark* from Revelation 13:16-17 is translated from the Greek word *charagma* meaning a brand, tattoo or stamp as a badge of servitude (Strong's *Exhaustive Concordance of the Bible*, p. 5480 in the Greek Testament). The number 666 written in Greek creates a very different impression from what we see in English. The first number pronounced "khee" appears as a fallen cross. The second number pronounced "xee" appears like a coiled serpent and the last number pronounced "stigma" also has a meaning as a word in Greek of a mark incised or punched into for a mark of ownership (ibid., p. 78 #5516). In English the word *stigma* also means a mark of disgrace or infamy.

5516. Χξ͞ς **chi xi stigma**, *khee xee stig'-ma*; the 22d, 14th and an obsl. letter (*4742* as a cross) of the Greek alphabet (intermediate between the 5th and 6th), used as numbers; denoting respectively 600, 60 and 6; 666 as a numeral:--six hundred threescore and six.

So there, in three symbols, we have a summation of the goals of socialism: to push over Christianity, to exalt the serpent, and to control economically the buying and selling through marking everyone as its slave. Other interpretations of the number 666 may also apply.

In the sixteenth chapter of Revelation we are introduced to the **fifth** character. This entity is referred to as three unclean spirits like frogs (Revelation 16:13). Frogs live a dual life. Above the surface frogs appear very differently than the way they act below the surface. This entity comes out of the mouth of the dragon (Satan), out of the mouth of the beast (communism), and out of the mouth of the false prophet (Karl Marx). They go forth to the kings of the earth, the end result being the whole world is gathered to battle (Revelation 16:14).

With all this understanding in place, we are now shown into the very heart of the satanic conspiracy. John has seen such an array of evil power that he marvels (Revelation 17:6-7). The **_sixth_** and last entity is named the great whore and upon her forehead was the name written MYSTERY, BABYLON THE GREAT, THE MOTHER OF HARLOTS, AND THE ABOMINATIONS OF THE EARTH (Revelation 17:1, 17:5). Now compare what is described here with what serious scholars of world events know of the internationalists who control the world's banking and money systems. The revelator sees that the whore sitteth upon many waters (Revelation 17:1) which is given the interpretation to mean peoples, multitudes, nations, and tongues (Revelation 17:15). We see that her power begins with her fornication with the kings of the earth and ends with her reigning over them (Revelation 17:2, 17:18). We see that the whore gets her control from the wine of her fornications held in a golden cup in which the inhabitants of the earth have been made drunk (Revelation 17:2, 17:4). The revelation does not tell us what the wine is, but the answer was given centuries earlier by the prophet Isaiah in the very first and most politically relevant chapter of his revelation. Isaiah tells us that he is talking about the whore: "How is the faithful city become a harlot! It was full of judgment; righteousness lodged in it; but now murderers" (Isaiah 1:21). Then Isaiah clearly tells us that the wine is currency and credit: "Thy silver is become dross, thy wine mixed with water" (Isaiah 1:22). When we understand what has caused our silver coins (legal money according to our Constitution) to be replaced with dross (base metals) and the process of inflation (mixing the wine with water), then we also understand the whore. Isaiah teaches that the people are drunk but not with wine; they stagger but not with strong drink; they are in the spirit of a deep drunken sleep (Isaiah 29:9-10). Can we see the world following the whore, seeking immediate gratification like drunkenness,

147

pursuing debt like addiction, losing its morals and closing its eyes to the evil like the spirit of the deep sleep? Like the revelation of John, Isaiah also tells us of a happy day after the cleansing.

What is the whore's fornication with the kings of the earth? Consider the Federal Reserve Act as a violation of the marriage covenant between the people and our government. Congress was told through this act they no longer needed to rely on the people for their source of money, but could borrow all they required from a central bank in the people's name. What have been the fruits of the Federal Reserve? The system only works because our freedom is sold by the commitment to collect an unfair, unequal, previously unconstitutional direct tax. Even more sinister, however, is the creation of war as a means to increase indebtedness and control. The Revelator sees the whore drunk with the blood of saints and with the blood of the martyrs of Jesus (Revelation 17:6). This teaches that those who have died for freedom have died for God, but it also tells us who is behind this shedding of blood.

To understand what finally becomes of the whore, we must also see what her relationship is to the scarlet beast (communism). We first see her sitting upon the scarlet colored beast (Revelation 17:3). We know now from the diligent work of many researchers that these internationalists established, built up, supported and fed the communistic movement for profit and to further their cause of global control. Like the old horror movie where the mad scientist creates the new life without the wisdom to govern it, the Revelator tells us these shall hate the whore, and shall make her desolate and naked and shall eat her flesh and burn her with fire (Revelation 17:16). And what of the good guys? The Book of Revelation is full of wonderful promises. We are up to the challenges. "These shall make war with the Lamb and the Lamb shall overcome them; for He is Lord of Lords, and King of Kings: and they that are with Him are called and chosen and faithful" (Revelation 17:14).

Once we see the great evil exposed, then the question to be answered is "whom will ye serve . . .? As for me and my house we shall serve the Lord" (Joshua 24:15). At this point the whore

Babylon is ready to be burned. The righteous are commanded to come out of her that they be not partakers of her plagues. The Savior Himself will tread the winepress that will be flowing with blood (Revelation 14:19, 19:15).

When John is shown this great latter-day combination of evil, he marvels.

Synopsis of the Seven Plagues

Once we have recognized the evil, then we see more clearly the nature and order the seven great last-day plagues or challenges that come upon the earth. These plagues could hardly be stated in more concise terms than presented by John. They are even numbered. John also shows us that they appear differently to different groups of people.

In synopsis this author believes we are being told that they will begin with a conventional war with modern weapons and bloodshed. Next is an escalation to the use of weapons of mass destruction in a naval conflict. This is the early warning needed to see when to button down the hatches, so to speak. Following is the use of nuclear weapons on the land. People are dying more because they are not protected from the bitterness (radioactive iodine) than from the impact of "the great star from heaven, burning as it were a lamp". This is followed by a darkening of the sun and sky (aftermath of the burning). The world is then plagued by a wicked world leader who is so tyrannical that his subjects wish for death but cannot find it. He has gained his power because he tells the people he will save every green thing. The good news is that we are told twice by John that his reign will only last for five months. With all this destruction, an army of 200 million soldiers will begin moving like locusts. Locusts move because they are hungry and so it is with this army. Then comes the finale which destroys the wicked and delivers the righteous. For details see chapters 8 and 9 an 18 of the Book of Revelation.

This Author believes that while terrible destruction is decreed for our day, so also is deliverance for those who have heeded the Biblical message of John. Knowing the timing may allow us to be gathered into shelter (the wheat and tares parable, Matthew 13:24-30) and partake of a type of a modern Passover.

Appendix B

Freedom vs. non Freedom: a view from Russia. This article (used by permission from Imprimis Jan. 2007, adapted from a speech at Hillsdale College National Leadership Seminar .) is included in this book because what is currently occurring politically in Russia is going to affect us. Some in the media are saying that freedom and liberty did not work in Russia. This inside view illustrates that it did not work because it was never tried. Andrei Illarionov, is the former chief economic advisor to the President of the Russian Federation. He has held this position twice, and resigned both times in protest of government policies. Dr. Illarionov is the author of three books, and over 300 articles, and is currently the President of the Institute of Economic Analysis in Moscow.

Constitutionalism in the Western political tradition does not mean-as it does in my own country, Russia-simply having a written constitution, regardless of its content. Rather, true constitutionalism requires the limitation of government by law. A government can be considered genuinely constitutional only if it operates under the following minimal constraints: (1) The legislature cannot be dismissed by any body or person other than itself. (2) The courts are independent of the legislative and executive branches. (3) The executive branch cannot appoint ministers without the approval of the legislative branch. (4) Only the legislature can pass laws.

It is not easy to find indications of such constitutionalism in my country. Our legislative branch, the Parliament, was dissolved in October 1993 by presidential decree. And for those who did not fully understand or immediately agree with that decree, some quite convincing tank shells were fired on the Parliament building. Russian courts are probably independent of the legislative branch, but they are completely subordinate to the executive. Ministers are simply appointed by the president. And while it is true that the legislature formally makes laws, the fact is that in the last seven years, there has not been a single executive desire that the Parliament has not passed into law. Thus it is not quite right to say, as some do, that constitutionalism is failing in Russia. In truth, Russia has yet to attempt it.

Why is this important? The answer is simple: constitutionalism is the best way, the most efficient way, and in fact the only way, to secure freedom.

"Freedom is not a luxury"

It is always worth pausing to refresh our memories-as well as the memories of our friends, colleagues, and even our adversaries-concerning the reasons why freedom is better than non-freedom.

Freedom is not a luxury. It is a very powerful instrument, without which no person and no country in the world can have sustained prosperity, security, development or respect. Free countries are certainly more prosperous than non-free countries. The Heritage Foundation's Index of Economic Freedom, the Fraser Institute's Economic Freedom of the World, and Freedom House's Freedom in the World all provide overwhelming evidence that economically and politically free countries are much richer than non-free countries-with a GDP per capita, on average, between $28,000 and $30,000, compared to approximately $4,000 per person in non-free or repressed countries.

In addition, the economies of free countries grow faster. During the past 30 years, completely free countries doubled per capita income, and partially free countries increased per capita income 40 percent on average. By contrast, non-free countries reduced per capita income roughly 34 percent. Over the same period, several countries changed their status from political freedom to political non-freedom, and others from political non-freedom to political freedom. The former change leads inevitably to economic degradation, resulting in a negative GDP per capita growth rate. The transition from non-freedom to freedom, on the other hand, speeds up economic growth, resulting in a GDP per capita growth rate higher than the world average.

Freedom also provides security. This is true for external security, because economically and politically free countries are less likely to fight each other than are non-free countries; it is also true for domestic security, as free countries usually have lower mortality rates from violent crime committed by criminal gangs or by the government. Compare the United States, Western Europe, Canada, and Japan on the one hand, and non-free countries like Rwanda, Afghanistan, Iraq, Somalia, and North Korea on the other. Which countries are more secure? Where is the life expectancy higher? Where is there a greater risk of robbery, kidnapping or murder?

Related to this, freedom enhances economic, political and military strength. Let's compare countries with similar population sizes but different levels of freedom. Which are economically more powerful? Spain or Sudan? Australia or Syria? Belgium or Cuba? Canada or Myanmar? The Netherlands or Zimbabwe? Taiwan or North Korea? Finland or Libya? Freedom also leads to greater international respect: Which of these countries is considered more attractive and more respected in the world? To which do people immigrate? From which do people emigrate? People vote for freedom with their feet.

The lack of freedom, on the other hand, creates an insurmountable barrier to prosperity and economic growth. For instance, there are no examples in world history of non-free countries that in a sustained way overcame a GDP per capita barrier of $15,000. Countries that have been able to cross this barrier did so only when they became free, politically and economically. Spain, Portugal, Greece, Taiwan, South Korea and Chile are among the best known examples of such a transition. Relatedly, countries that were rich but became non-free, also became poor-even oil-exporting countries in years of high energy prices. In Iran, Venezuela, Saudi Arabia and Iraq, the GDP per capita today is lower than it was three decades ago, by 10, 30, 40 and 80 percent, respectively. The lack of freedom always destroys wealth.

The Destruction of Freedom in Russia

The story of the destruction of freedom in my own country, Russia, is sad. But this story should be told, should be known, and should be remembered-to avoid repeating it and in order one day to reverse it.

First, there was an assault on the people of Chechnya. Many Russian people thought that it was not their business to defend the freedom of the Chechen people. People in Chechnya lost their independence, their political rights and-many of them-their lives. Many Russians lost their lives as well.

Then there was an assault on the Russian media. This time many Russian people thought that it was not their business to defend the freedom of the media. As a result, the media lost its independence-first television channels, then radio stations and newspapers. And now the censors are turning their attention to the Internet.

Then there was an assault on private business. Many Russian people thought that it was not their business to defend the freedom of private business. So private business has lost its independence and has become subjugated to the caprice of the executive power. This has been accomplished through so-called PPPs or public-private partnerships, but it would be more correct to call what is happening CPC-coercion of private business by the corporation in power.

Then there was an assault on the independence of political parties. Many Russian people thought that it was not their business to defend the independence of political parties. As a result, independent national political parties ceased to exist.

Then there was an assault on the independence of the judiciary. Many Russian people thought that it was not their business to defend the independence of the judiciary. Now, there are no more independent courts or judges in Russia.

Then there was an assault on the election of regional governors. Many Russian people thought that it was not their business to defend free elections of regional governors. Today, regional governors are appointed by the president, and there are no more independent regional authorities in the country.

Then there was an assault on the independence of non-governmental and religious organizations. Finally, some people tried to defend the freedom of these organizations, but it was too late. And now even those who want to resist have neither the resources nor the institutions required to fight back.

As a result, Russia has ceased to be politically free. For 2005, Freedom House's Freedom in the World ranks Russia 168th out of 192 countries. Transparency International's Global Corruption Report ranks Russia 126th out of 159 countries. The World Economic Forum calculates that Russia is 85th (among 108 countries) in avoiding favoritism in government decisions, 88th (also of 108) in its protection of property rights, and 84th (of 102) when measured by the independence of the judicial system. The Russian government could form another G-8 with countries that destroyed the fundamental institutions of modern government and civil society as quickly as it did over the past 15 years by partnering with Nepal, Belarus, Tajikistan, Gambia, the Solomon Islands, Zimbabwe and Venezuela.

What is the Russian government doing now, when it has destroyed freedom and achieved next to full control over Russian society? Is it stopping its assaults? No. It continues them, both within and beyond Russia's borders. Inside the country, the government has started a campaign against human rights. It has created and financed detachments of storm troopers-the movements "Nashi" ("Our Own"), "Mestnye" ("Locals"), and "Molodaya gvardiya" ("Young Guard")-which are being taught and trained to harass and beat political and intellectual opponents of the current regime. The days for which these storm troopers are especially trained will come soon-during the parliamentary and presidential elections in 2007 and 2008.

Beyond Russia's national borders, the government provides economic, financial, political, intellectual and moral support to new friends: leaders of non-free countries such as Belarus, Uzbekistan, Venezuela, Myanmar, Algeria, Iran, and Palestinian Hamas. At the same time, Russia is attempting to destroy hard-won freedom and democracy in neighboring countries. Ukraine, Moldova and Georgia find themselves in a new cold war as Russian authorities pursue hostile policies involving visas, poultry imports, electricity, natural gas, pipelines, wine, and even mineral water. The Russian government has just started a full-scale blockade of Georgia. Meanwhile, the state-controlled Russian media has launched a propaganda war against Ukraine, Moldova, Georgia, the Baltic countries, Europe and the United States.

What do non-free countries have in common? What unites such disparate countries as Nepal, Belarus, Tajikistan, the Solomon Islands, Gambia, Venezuela, Zimbabwe, North Korea, Sudan, Turkmenistan, Cuba, Myanmar, and yes, now Russia? Only one thing: war, in which governments take away property and destroy society, in which they send people to camps or kill them solely because they have a different perception of the world, of faith, of law, and of their homeland. Only through hatred, fear, and electoral violence can these governments hold on to what is dearest to them-absolute power.

Without freedom there can be no open discussion of topics of national and international importance. There is an exclusion from public life of conversation about the most important matters. This primitivizes public life, degrades society, and weakens the state. The politics of non-freedom is the politics of public impoverishment and of the retardation of the country's economic growth.

The greatest practical lesson of Russia's recent history is that freedom is indivisible. The failure of freedom in one sphere makes it harder to defend freedom in other areas. Likewise, the fall of freedom in one country is a blow to global freedom. The inability to defend freedom yesterday comes back to haunt us at a great price today and perhaps an even greater price tomorrow.

Looking Ahead

What position should the United States and other free countries take regarding Russia's growing internal authoritarianism and external aggression? There was a real opportunity over the last several years: Concerted efforts by the West could have slowed significantly, if not stopped, the degradation of freedom in Russia. But nothing was done. One of the West's last chances was to deny access to its capital markets for the sale of assets stolen from the large private company Yukos; but this did not happen, and the sale of those assets occurred at the Rosneft IPO on the London Stock Exchange. The July 2006 G-8 summit in St. Petersburg could also have been used to emphasize the clear distinction between leaders of the free world and those of non-free Russia. But in the end, nothing was done.

As I wrote in the Washington Post in April 2006:

The G-8 summit can only be interpreted as a sign of support by the world's most powerful organization for Russia's leadership-as a stamp of approval for its violations of individual rights, the rule of law and freedom of speech, its discrimination against nongovernmental organizations, nationalization of private property, use of energy resources as a weapon, and aggression toward democratically oriented neighbors.

By going to St. Petersburg, leaders of the world's foremost industrialized democracies will demonstrate their indifference to the fate of freedom and democracy in Russia. They will provide the best possible confirmation of what the Russian authorities never tire of repeating: that there are no fundamental differences between Western and Russian leaders. Like us, Russia's leaders will say, they are interested only in

155

appearing to care about the rights of individuals and market forces; like us, they only talk about freedom and democracy. The G-8 summit will serve as an inspiring example for today's dictators and tomorrow's tyrants.

The West squandered both of these opportunities. None of the G-7 leaders had enough courage to raise the issues of freedom and democracy, or to discuss the principles of true constitutionalism and their absence in Russia. Everyone pretended that nothing special was going on in Russia. Indeed, the G-7 leaders agreed de facto with the Russian authorities' approach to energy security. Instead of liberalizing and privatizing energy assets, Russia is moving in the opposite direction both internally-by nationalizing private companies and asserting state control over the electricity grid and pipeline system-and internationally, by using non-market methods to manage supply and even demand for the world's energy resources.

Several months after the summit, the bill for this policy of appeasement is due. Now the Russian authorities are revoking the licenses of American and British energy companies in Sakhalin. BP has found itself under pressure to exchange its partner in TNK-BP in favor of the government-owned Gazprom. Otherwise, it will not have a chance to explore the giant Kovykta gas field in eastern Siberia. The billion dollars it spent on the purchase of Rosneft shares in July 2006 did not help BP much. And there is no doubt that, after the G-8 summit, the free world can expect more of the same. In truth, it should consider itself in a new Cold War-like era.

* * *

Let me conclude these remarks with words spoken by Winston Churchill about another great war for freedom:

I would say to the House, as I said to those who have joined this government: "I have nothing to offer but blood, toil, tears and sweat." We have before us an ordeal of the most grievous kind. We have before us many, many long months of struggle and of suffering. You ask, what is our policy? I can say: It is to wage war, by sea, land and air, with all our might and with all the strength that God can give us; to wage war against a monstrous tyranny, never surpassed in the dark, lamentable catalogue of human crime. That is our policy. You ask, what is our aim? I can answer in one word: It is victory, victory at all costs, victory in spite of all terror, victory, however long and hard the road may be; for without victory, there is no survival.

That war for freedom was won. We may yet win, indeed we must win, this current war. But to win, we must work together.